PRIMARY MATHEMATICS

TEXTBOOK 3B

Common Core Edition

SINGAPORE MATH® PROGRAM

Marshall Cavendish Education

US Distributor

SM Singapore Math Inc.®

BLANK

Original edition published under the title Primary Mathematics Textbook 3B
© 1981 Curriculum Planning & Development Division, Ministry of Education, Singapore
Published by Times Media Private Limited

This edition © 2014 Marshall Cavendish Education Pte Ltd
(Formerly known as Marshall Cavendish International (Singapore) Private Limited)

Published by Marshall Cavendish Education
Times Centre, 1 New Industrial Road, Singapore 536196
Customer Service Hotline: (65) 6213 9444
US Office Tel: (1-914) 332 8888 | Fax: (1-914) 332 8882
E-mail: tmesales@mceducation.com
Website: www.mceducation.com

Distributed by
Singapore Math Inc.®
19535 WS 129th Avenue
Tualatin, OR 97062
Tel: (503) 557 8100
Website: www.singaporemath.com

First published 2014

Singapore Math® is a trademark of Singapore Math Inc.® and
Marshall Cavendish Education Pte Ltd.

Primary Mathematics (Common Core Edition) Textbook 3B
ISBN 978-981-01-9834-3

Printed in Singapore

Primary Mathematics (Common Core Edition) is adapted from Primary Mathematics Textbook 3B (3rd Edition), originally developed by the Ministry of Education, Singapore. This edition contains new content developed by Marshall Cavendish Education Pte Ltd, which is not attributable to the Ministry of Education, Singapore.

We would like to acknowledge the contributions by:

The Project Team from the Ministry of Education, Singapore, that developed the original Singapore Edition
Project Director: Dr Kho Tek Hong
Team Members: Hector Chee Kum Hoong, Liang Hin Hoon, Lim Eng Tann, Ng Siew Lee, Rosalind Lim Hui Cheng, Ng Hwee Wan

Primary Mathematics (Common Core Edition)
Richard Askey, Emeritus Professor of Mathematics from University of Wisconsin, Madison
Jennifer Kempe, Curriculum Advisor from Singapore Math Inc.®

PREFACE

PRIMARY MATHEMATICS Common Core Edition is a complete program from Marshall Cavendish Education, the publisher of Singapore's successful *Primary Mathematics* series. Newly adapted to align with the Common Core State Standards for mathematics, the program aims to equip students with sound concept development, critical thinking and efficient problem-solving skills.

Mathematical concepts are introduced in the opening pages and taught to mastery through specific learning tasks that allow for immediate assessment and consolidation.

The **modeling method** enables students to visualize and solve mathematical problems quickly and efficiently.

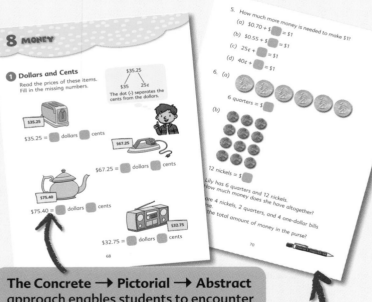

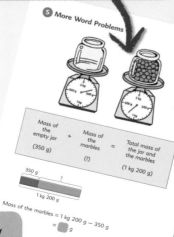

The Concrete → Pictorial → Abstract approach enables students to encounter math in a meaningful way and translate mathematical skills from the concrete to the abstract.

The **pencil icon** ✏️ Exercise 1, pages 63–64 provides quick and easy reference from the Textbook to the relevant Workbook pages. The **direct correlation** of the Workbook to the Textbook facilitates focused review and evaluation.

New mathematical concepts are introduced through a **spiral progression** that builds on concepts already taught and mastered.

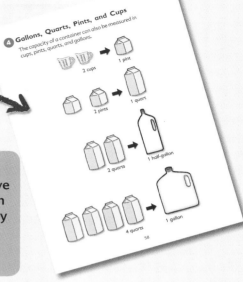

4 Gallons, Quarts, Pints, and Cups

The capacity of a container can also be measured in cups, pints, quarts, and gallons.

2 cups → 1 pint

2 pints → 1 quart

2 quarts → 1 half-gallon

4 quarts → 1 gallon

58

The color patch is used to invite active student participation and to facilitate lively discussion about the mathematical concepts taught.

16. Fill in the blanks.

9:10   10:00   12:00 midnight   4:00
P.M.   P.M.   A.M.

(a) 4:00 A.M. is ☐ h after 12:00 midnight.
(b) 6:40 A.M. is ☐ h ☐ min after 12:00 midnight.
(c) 9:10 P.M. is ☐ h ☐ min before 12:00 midnight.

17. A night tour began at 10:30 P.M. and lasted 3 h 20 min. When did the night tour end?

3 h 20 min

30 min   1h   ?   A.M.

10:30 P.M.   11:00 P.M.   12:00 midnight

— 1 h → 2 h 20 min — 30 min → 1 h 50 min

3 h 20 min

3 h 20 min — 1 h 30 min = ☐ h ☐ min

The night tour ended at ☐ A.M.

18. Add or subtract.
(a) 2 h 40 min + 3 h
(b) 2 h 20 min + 45 min
(c) 3 h 15 min — 2 h
(d) 3 h 5 min — 30 min
(e) 1 h 25 min + 2 h 15 min
(f) 2 h 40 min + 2 h 25 min
(g) 3 h 50 min — 1 h 35 min
(h) 3 h 20 min + 1 h 40 min

119

Metacognition is employed as a strategy for learners to monitor their thinking processes in problem solving. Speech and thought bubbles provide guidance through the thought processes, making even the most challenging problems accessible to students.

REVIEW 8

1. Which amount is the greatest?
   (A) 25 dimes   (B) 80 nickels
   (C) 2 dollars   (D) 10 quarters

2. Fourteen dollars and seven cents is the same as _____
   (A) $14.07   (B) $14.70
   (C) $40.07   (D) $40.70

3. 1,050¢ = _____
   (A) $10.05   (B) $10.50
   (C) $105.00   (D) $100.50

4. Livia received $30 from her father to buy a gift for her brother. The gift she bought cost $21.85. How much change did Livia receive after paying for the _____
   (A) $8.15   (B) $9.15
   (C) $11.15   (D) $18.15

5. Select True or False.
   (a) $1 = 1,000¢   True / False
   (b) 245¢ + 475¢ > 700¢   True / False

6. Select True or False.
   (a) $83 < $81.25 + $0.85   True / False
   (b) $47.45 + $0.95 = $47.45 + $1 − $0.05   True / False

7. Write each amount of money in words.
   (a) $1.48   (b) $30.60
   (c) $35.75   (d) $94.05

B1

Regular **reviews** in the Textbook provide consolidation of concepts learned.

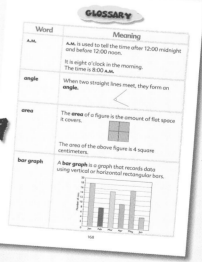

GLOSSARY

Word	Meaning
A.M.	A.M. is used to tell the time after 12:00 midnight and before 12:00 noon. It is eight o'clock in the morning. The time is 8:00 A.M.
angle	When two straight lines meet, they form an **angle**.
area	The **area** of a figure is the amount of flat space it covers. The area of the above figure is 4 square centimeters.
bar graph	A **bar graph** is a graph that records data using vertical or horizontal rectangular bars.

168

The **Glossary** effectively combines pictorial representation with simple mathematical definitions to provide a comprehensive reference guide for students.

CONTENTS

6 MASS AND WEIGHT

1 Comparing Mass

The watermelon is **as heavy as** the dictionary.

The loaf of bread is **lighter** than the carton of milk.

The carton of milk is **heavier** than the loaf of bread.

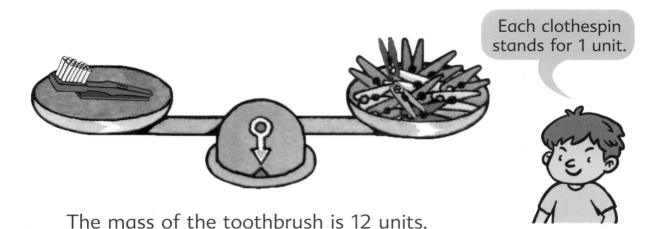

Each clothespin stands for 1 unit.

The mass of the toothbrush is 12 units.

Each marble stands for 1 unit.

The mass of the toothbrush is 10 units.

Which is greater, the number of clothespin units or the number of marble units?

Which is lighter, a clothespin or a marble?

Exercise 1, pages 7–8

2 Measuring Mass in Kilograms

Hold a 1-kilogram mass in your hand.
Feel how heavy it is.

The **kilogram** is a unit of mass.
We write **kg** for kilogram.

The mass of the book is less than 1 kg. It is lighter than 1 kg.

The bag has a mass greater than 1 kg. It is heavier than 1 kg.
Is the bag heavier or lighter than the book?

1. Fill a bag with beans so that it has a mass of 1 kg.

2. Look for some objects that have a mass of about 1 kg.

3. The mass of the suitcase is

    kg.

4. Find an object that you think has a mass of about 4 kg. Measure its mass.

5. Estimate your mass in kilograms and then measure it.

6.

(a) Which package is heavier?

(b) How much heavier?

(c) What is the total mass of the two packages?

7.

(a) Which toolbox is the heaviest?

(b) Which toolbox is the lightest?

(c) What is the total mass of the three toolboxes?

8. Raj has a mass of 39 kg.

His father is 28 kg heavier than he is.

Find the mass of Raj's father.

9. The mass of a sheep is 262 kg.

The mass of a goat is 129 kg.

How much lighter is the goat than the sheep?

10. Brian's mass is 60 kg.
He is 5 times as heavy as his son.
How many kilograms does Brian's son weigh?

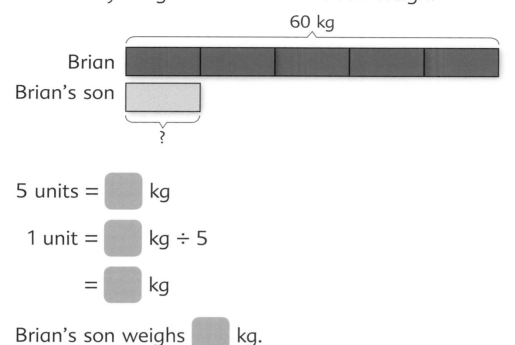

5 units = ☐ kg

1 unit = ☐ kg ÷ 5

= ☐ kg

Brian's son weighs ☐ kg.

11. Kumar had 820 kg of rice. He distributed the rice equally to 10 food banks. How much rice did each food bank get?

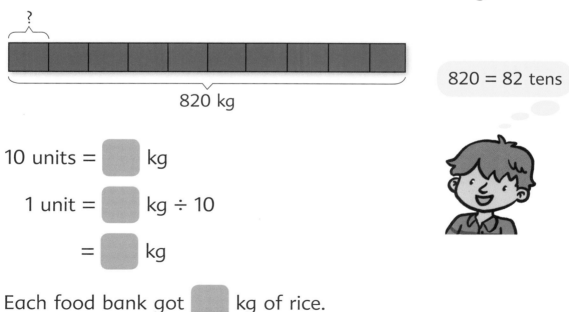

820 = 82 tens

10 units = ☐ kg

1 unit = ☐ kg ÷ 10

= ☐ kg

Each food bank got ☐ kg of rice.

12. A restaurant throws away 8 kg of leftovers each week.
    What is the total mass of leftovers thrown away in 6 weeks?

8 kg

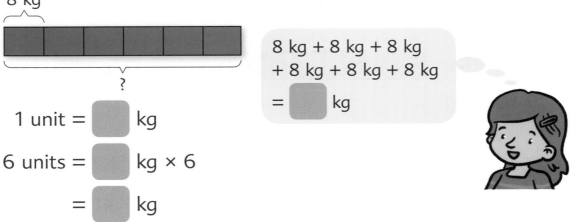

1 unit = ☐ kg

6 units = ☐ kg × 6

= ☐ kg

8 kg + 8 kg + 8 kg
+ 8 kg + 8 kg + 8 kg

= ☐ kg

The total mass of leftovers thrown away in 6 weeks is ☐ kg.

13. Linda has a mass of 32 kg now.
    She was twice as heavy five years ago.
    How heavy was Linda five years ago?

14. Mr. Flint wants to pack 3 kg of fruit in each of 7 boxes.
    What is the total mass of the fruit he has to pack?

15. A fast food outlet sells 45 kg of chips each week.
    How many kilograms of chips can the outlet sell in 4 weeks?

16. Malcolm bought 18 kg of hamburger meat last month.
    He plans to buy twice as much hamburger meat this month.
    How many kilograms of hamburger meat does he plan to
    buy this month?

17. Bjork has 460 kg of dog food.
    He wants to pack the food equally into bags of 2 kg.
    How many bags can he pack?

18. Mrs. Taylor bought 810 kg of flour.
    She uses 3 kg of flour a week to bake muffins.
    How many weeks can the flour last for?

Exercise 2, pages 9—12

3 Measuring Mass in Grams

The **gram** is another unit of mass.
We write **g** for gram.
1,000 g = 1 kg

Find some of these objects and feel how heavy they are.

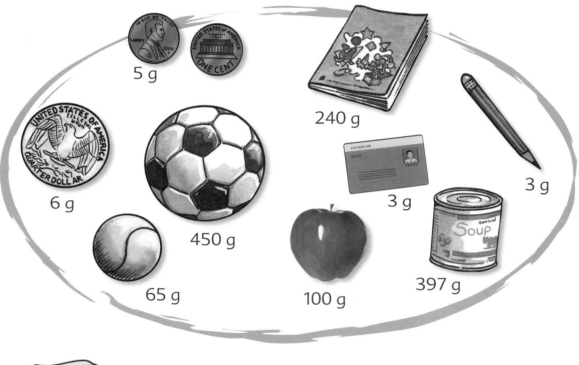

5 g

240 g

3 g

6 g

450 g

3 g

65 g

100 g

397 g

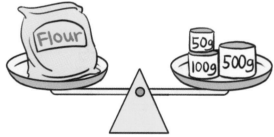

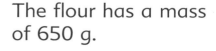

The flour has a mass of 650 g.

The grapes have a mass of 632 g.

1. Measure the mass of some objects in grams.

A pair of scissors   A pen   A notebook

2. Fill in the blanks.

(a)

The carrots have a mass of [ ] g.

(b)

The potatoes have a mass of [ ] g.

(c) Together, the potatoes and the carrots have a mass of [ ] g.

3. Fill in the blanks.

(a)

The mushrooms have a mass of [ ] g.

(b)

The lettuce leaves have a mass of [ ] g.

(c) Which is heavier, the mushrooms or the lettuce leaves?
(d) How much heavier?

4.

674 g is about 700 g.
253 g is about 300 g.

700 g + 300 g = 1,000 g

The answer is reasonable if it is about 1,000 g.

Mr. Siva bought 674 g of potatoes and 253 g of onions.
What is the total mass of the potatoes and onions?

5. A bottle of sauce has a mass of 560 g.
The empty bottle has a mass of 305 g.
How many grams of sauce are there in the bottle?

6. A lobster has a mass of 900 g.
A crab has a mass of 550 g.
(a) Which is heavier, the lobster or the crab?
(b) How much heavier?

7. Betty used 155 g of sugar to bake some cookies.
She had 245 g left.
How much sugar did she have at first?

8. A basketball has a mass of 535 g.
A soccer ball has a mass of 420 g.
How much lighter is the soccer ball than the basketball?

9. A math textbook has a mass of 462 g.
Its mass is 395 g less than the mass of a dictionary.
What is the mass of the dictionary?

10. Lewis bought 800 g of pasta.
He used some to make his dinner and had 205 g left.
How much pasta did he use for his dinner?

11. Samantha bought 500 g of grapes each day for a week.
    What is the total mass of grapes she bought over 7 days?

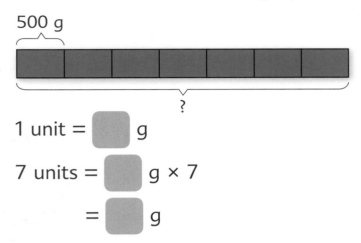

500 g

?

1 unit = ☐ g

7 units = ☐ g × 7

= ☐ g

The total mass of grapes she bought over 7 days is ☐ g.

12. The mass of a pack of jelly beans is 510 g.
    It is three times as heavy as a bag of chips.
    What is the mass of a bag of chips?

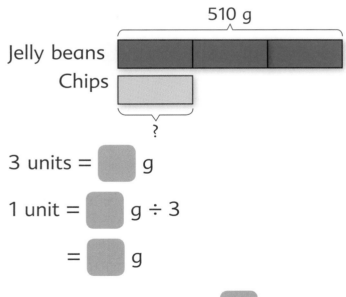

510 g

Jelly beans

Chips

?

3 units = ☐ g

1 unit = ☐ g ÷ 3

= ☐ g

A bag of chips weighs ☐ g.

13. Mrs. Kim packs 180 g of carrots for each of her children's lunchboxes.
She has 4 children.
How many grams of carrots does she have to pack in all?

14. Sammi prepares 8 identical piñatas.
Each piñatas weighs 300 g.
What is the total mass of the piñatas?

15. Mr. Fay eats 20 g of vitamins each day.
Mrs. Fay eats three times as many vitamins each day.
How many vitamins does Mrs. Fay eat each day?

16. Eleanor made 250 g of pasta.
She made potato salad that was twice as heavy as the pasta.
What is the mass of the potato salad that she made?

17. Carl bought 960 g of prawns this week.
He bought three times as much prawns as last week.
How many grams of prawns did he buy last week?

18. The total mass of 5 jars of peanut butter is 850 g.
Find the mass of 1 jar of peanut butter.

19. The total mass of 9 tennis balls is 540 g.
What is the mass of 1 tennis ball?

20. 8 tubes of toothpaste have a mass of 520 g altogether.
What is the mass of 1 tube of toothpaste?

21. Dr. Clark eats 980 g of vegetables every week.
How many grams of vegetables does he eat each day?

Exercise 3, pages 13—16

4 Kilograms and Grams

Complete the sentences.

1.

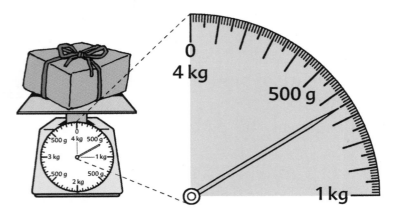

The package has a mass of g.

2.

The grapes have a mass of   The pumpkin has a mass of

 g.   kg g.

3.

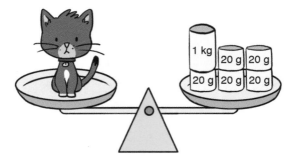

The kitten has a mass of 1 kg g.

4. Read the scales.

(a)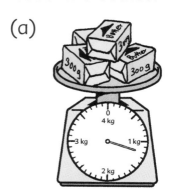

(b)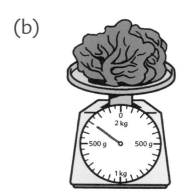

Exercise 4, page 17

5. The potatoes have a mass of 2 kg 200 g.
   Write the mass in grams.

2 kg = 2,000 g

6. Write in grams.
   (a) 1 kg 456 g   (b) 2 kg 370 g   (c) 3 kg 808 g
   (d) 2 kg 80 g   (e) 1 kg 8 g   (f) 4 kg 7 g

7. Each book has a mass of 250 g.
   The total mass of the 4 books

   is ☐ kg ☐ g.

8. Write in kilograms and grams.
   (a) 2,143 g   (b) 1,354 g   (c) 3,800 g
   (d) 2,206 g   (e) 3,085 g   (f) 4,009 g

9.

1,100 g   **1 kg 250 g**

Which is heavier, the fish or the chicken?
How much heavier?

Exercise 5, pages 18—20

10. A bag of peanuts has a mass of 1 kg 850 g.
    How many more grams are needed to make 2 kg?

1 kg − 850 g = ▢ g

2 kg − 1 kg 850 g = ▢ g

11. Find the missing numbers.

(a) 1 kg − 395 g = ▢ g

(b) 1 kg − 85 g = ▢ g

(c) 3 kg − 2 kg 400 g = ▢ g

(d) 5 kg − 4 kg 60 g = ▢ g

(e) 1 kg − 540 g = ▢ g

(f) 3 kg − 805 g = ▢ kg ▢ g

12.

3 kg 80 g   **1 kg 960 g**

(a) Find the total mass of the watermelon and the bananas.

3 kg 80 g + 1 kg 960 g = ▢ kg ▢ g

3 kg 80 g $\xrightarrow{+1\,kg}$ 4 kg 80 g $\xrightarrow{+960\,g}$ 5 kg 40 g

The total mass is ▢ kg ▢ g.

(b) Find the difference in mass between the watermelon and the bananas.

3 kg 80 g − 1 kg 960 g = ▢ kg ▢ g

3 kg 80 g $\xrightarrow{-1\,kg}$ 2 kg 80 g $\xrightarrow{-960\,g}$ 1 kg 120 g

The difference in mass is ▢ kg ▢ g.

13.

Onions

2 kg 600 g

Tomatoes

1 kg 500 g

(a) What is the total mass of the onions and the tomatoes?

(b) What is the difference in mass between the onions and the tomatoes?

14. Add or subtract in compound units.

(a) 3 kg 500 g + 2 kg   (b) 4 kg 650 g + 450 g

(c) 3 kg 100 g + 1 kg 900 g (d) 2 kg 50 g + 4 kg 70 g

(e) 3 kg 10 g − 200 g   (f) 4 kg 300 g − 1 kg 50 g

(g) 4 kg 250 g − 1 kg 500 g (h) 5 kg − 2 kg 905 g

15. Lily had a mass of 25 kg 750 g two years ago.
Now she has a mass of 32 kg.
How much mass did she gain?

16. A pumpkin has a mass of 2 kg 990 g.
A watermelon has a mass of 4 kg 200 g.

(a) Find the total mass of the pumpkin and the watermelon.

(b) Find the difference in mass between the pumpkin and the watermelon.

Exercise 6, pages 21–23

5 More Word Problems

What is the mass of the marbles?

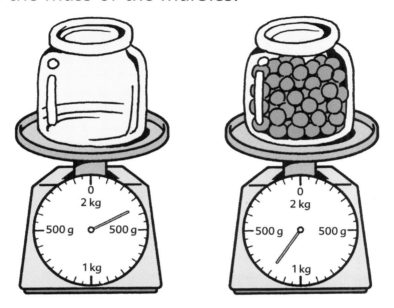

Mass of the empty jar	+	Mass of the marbles	=	Total mass of the jar and the marbles
(350 g)		(?)		(1 kg 200 g)

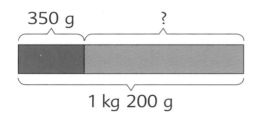

Mass of the marbles = 1 kg 200 g − 350 g

= ⬜ g

1. A box of canned soup has a mass of 1 kg 560 g.
   The empty box has a mass of 305 g.
   What is the mass of the cans of soup in the box?

2. A washing machine has a mass of 78 kg 750 g.
   It is 12 kg 800 g lighter than a refrigerator.
   What is the mass of the refrigerator?

3. William has a mass of 57 kg.
   He is 3 times as heavy as Sean.
   What is the total mass
   of William and Sean?

   3 units = 57 kg

   1 unit = ⬜ kg ÷ 3 = ⬜ kg

   4 units = ⬜ kg × 4 = ⬜ kg

   The total mass of William and Sean is ⬜ kg.

4. John has a mass of 34 kg 600 g.
   He is 800 g heavier than David.
   What is David's mass?

   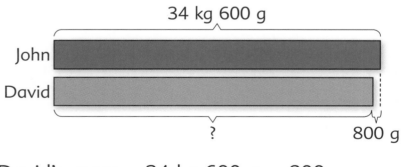

   David's mass = 34 kg 600 g − 800 g

   = ⬜ kg ⬜ g

5. The total mass of a football and 10 tennis balls is 1 kg 5 g. If the mass of each tennis ball is 60 g, find the mass of the football.

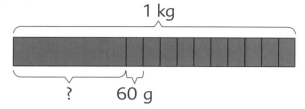

1 kg

?   60 g

Mass of 10 tennis balls = 60 × 10
= 600 g

Mass of the football = 1 kg 5 g − 600 g

= ⬚ g

The football has a mass of ⬚ g.

6. A watermelon is 5 times as heavy as a grapefruit.
The grapefruit has a mass of 950 g.
How much heavier is the watermelon than the grapefruit?

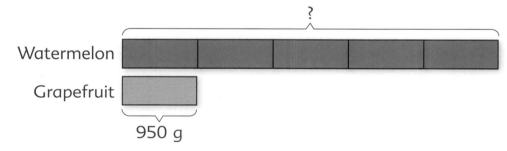

?

Watermelon

Grapefruit

950 g

1 unit = 950 g
Mass of watermelon = 5 units
The watermelon is 4 units heavier than the grapefruit.

4 units = ⬚ g = ⬚ kg ⬚ g

7. A goose has a mass of 3 kg 200 g.
A duck is 1 kg 400 g lighter than the goose.
What is the total mass of the goose and the duck?

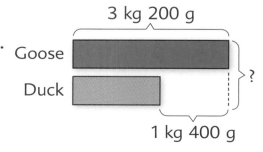

3 kg 200 g

Goose

Duck

?

1 kg 400 g

8. The total mass of a bottle of cooking oil and 2 bags of sugar is 5 kg 50 g.
If the mass of each bag of sugar is 2 kg, find the mass of the bottle of cooking oil.

Mass of 2 bags of sugar = ⬜ kg

Mass of the bottle of cooking oil = ⬜ kg ⬜ g

9. Fill in the blanks.
(a) Mass of the bag of rice = ⬜ kg

(b) The cost of the bag of rice is $5.

Cost of 1 kg of rice = $⬜

10. Fill in the blanks.
(a) Mass of the chicken = ⬜ kg

(b) Ms. King paid $6 for the chicken.

Cost of 1 kg of chicken = $⬜

11. Mr. Handyman bought 8 kg of nails for $24.
How much does 1 kg of nails cost?

Exercise 7, pages 24—26

6 Measuring Weight in Pounds and Ounces

> The **pound** is a unit of weight. We write **lb** for pound.

Hold a 1-pound weight in your hand. Feel how heavy it is.

1. Fill a bag with beans so that it weighs 1 pound.

Look for some objects that weigh about 1 pound.

2. Find your weight in pounds using a bathroom scale. Weigh some other things in pounds.

3. Use a balance.
   Compare a pound weight with a kilogram weight.

   Which is lighter?

4.

> The **ounce** is another unit of weight.
> We write **oz** for ounce.
> **16 oz = 1 lb**

8 oz

1 oz

16 oz

14 oz

2 oz

7 oz

   Use a balance and some ounce weights.
   Find the weight of some objects in ounces.

5. Use a balance. Compare an ounce with a gram.

Which is heavier?

6. Would you use pounds or ounces to weigh the following?

    (a) a horse _____

    (b) a mouse _____

    (c) a banana _____

    (d) a refrigerator _____

7. Mallory weighs 73 lb. Evie weighs 56 lb.

    (a) How much more does Mallory weigh than Evie?

    (b) How much do they both weigh?

8. A squirrel weighs 23 ounces. It is 18 ounces heavier than a chipmunk. How much does the chipmunk weigh?

Exercise 8, pages 27–28

9. Complete the sentences.

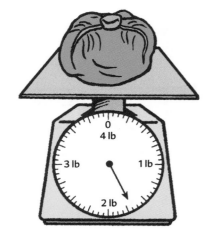

The mushrooms weigh

 oz.

The cabbage weighs

 lb oz.

10. The sack of flour weighs 4 lb 13 oz.
    Write the weight in oz.

1 lb = 1 × 16 = 16 oz
4 lb = 4 × 16 = 64 oz

11. Write in ounces.

   (a) 5 lb   (b) 7 lb 15 oz   (c) 9 lb 9 oz

12. Each stick of butter weighs 8 oz.
    The total weight of 3 sticks of

    butter is  lb  oz.

13. Write in pounds and ounces.

   (a) 16 oz   (b) 20 oz   (c) 26 oz

14. Find the difference between 1 lb and 14 oz.

1 lb − 14 oz =  oz   1 lb = 16 oz
16 oz − 14 oz = 2 oz

15. Find the difference between 3 lb and 10 oz.

1 lb − 10 oz = 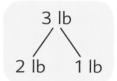 oz

3 lb − 10 oz = 2 lb  oz

3 lb
2 lb   1 lb

16. Find the sum of 12 oz and 9 oz.

12 oz + 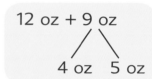 oz = 1 lb

12 oz + 9 oz = 1 lb  oz

12 oz + 9 oz
4 oz   5 oz

17. Find the missing numbers.

(a) 1 lb − 9 oz =  oz

(b) 5 lb − 4 oz = 4 lb ⬜ oz

(c) 14 oz + 10 oz = 1 lb ⬜ oz

(d) 3 lb 11 oz + 3 lb 6 oz = 7 lb ⬜ oz

(e) 10 lb − 3 oz = ⬜ lb ⬜ oz

(f) 2 lb 15 oz + 15 oz = ⬜ lb ⬜ oz

Exercise 9, pages 29–30

18.

1 lb 14 oz   **3 lb 9 oz**

(a) Find the total weight of the cantaloupe and
    the grapes.

3 lb 9 oz + 1 lb 14 oz = lb oz

3 lb 9 oz $\xrightarrow{+1\,lb}$ 4 lb 9 oz $\xrightarrow{+14\,oz}$ 5 lb 7 oz

The total weight is ___ lb ___ oz.

(b) Find the difference in weight between the cantaloupe
    and the grapes.

3 lb 9 oz − 1 lb 14 oz = ___ lb ___ oz

3 lb 9 oz $\xrightarrow{-1\,lb}$ 2 lb 9 oz $\xrightarrow{-14\,oz}$ 1 lb 11 oz

The difference in weight is ___ lb ___ oz.

19. Add or subtract.

    (a) 3 lb 12 oz + 5 lb 4 oz =  lb  oz

    (b) 12 lb 13 oz − 8 lb 10 oz = ☐ lb ☐ oz

    (c) 6 lb 9 oz + 5 lb 11 oz = ☐ lb ☐ oz

    (d) 12 lb 5 oz − 8 lb 10 oz = ☐ lb ☐ oz

20. The total weight of two watermelons
is 21 lb.
The bigger watermelon weighs
12 lb 9 oz.
What is the weight of the smaller watermelon?

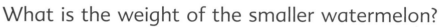

21.

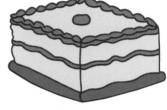
3 lb 7 oz

2 lb 10 oz

    (a) Find the total weight of the two cakes.

    (b) What is the difference in weight between the first cake and the second cake?

22. Hannah weighs 54 lb.
Her father is twice as heavy as her.
Her sister is 18 lb lighter than her father.

    (a) What is Hannah's father's weight?

    (b) What is her sister's weight?

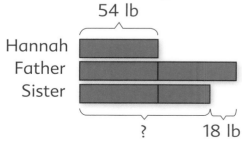

Exercise 10, pages 31–32

1.

How heavy is the can of soft drink?

(A) 300 g   (B) 320 g   (C) 350 g   (D) 370 g

2. 8 kg 3 g is the same as _____.

(A) 803 g   (B) 830 g   (C) 8,003 g   (D) 8,300 g

3. A paper clip has a mass of about _____.

(A) 1 g   (B) 10 g   (C) 50 g   (D) 100 g

4. Marcus used 105 g of minced beef to make a burger.
    He made 8 burgers.
    How much minced beef did he use?

(A) 113 g   (B) 120 g   (C) 840 g   (D) 845 g

5. Parcel A weighs 3 lb 2 oz.
    Parcel B weighs 1 lb 9 oz.
    How much heavier is Parcel A than Parcel B?

(A) 1 lb 3 oz

(B) 1 lb 9 oz

(C) 2 lb 3 oz

(D) 2 lb 7 oz

6. Select True or False.
   (a) 4 kg 30 g = 430 g   True / False
   (b) 2,000 g > 2 kg   True / False

7. Select True or False.
   (a) 5 lb 17 oz = 6 lb 1 oz   True / False
   (b) 38 oz > 2 lb 6 oz   True / False

8. Fill in the missing numbers.
   (a) 5 kg = ☐ g   (b) 1 kg 950 g = ☐ g

   (c) 1 kg 60 g = ☐ g   (d) 2 kg 805 g = ☐ g

   (e) 2 kg 5 g = ☐ g   (f) 3 kg 2 g = ☐ g

   (g) 1,905 g = ☐ kg ☐ g   (h) 1,055 g = ☐ kg ☐ g

   (i) 2,208 g = ☐ kg ☐ g   (j) 3,390 g = ☐ kg ☐ g

   (k) 3,599 g = ☐ kg ☐ g   (l) 5,002 g = ☐ kg ☐ g

9. Add or subtract in compound units.
   (a) 2 kg 940 g + 300 g   (b) 3 kg 880 g + 1 kg 220 g
   (c) 4 kg − 1 kg 480 g   (d) 5 kg 20 g − 2 kg 450 g
   (e) 4 kg 920 g + 125 g   (f) 3 kg 760 g + 4 kg 350 g
   (g) 6 kg − 4 kg 820 g   (h) 4 kg 25 g − 2 kg 230 g

10. Find the missing numbers.
    (a) 3 lb 2 oz = ☐ oz   (b) 4 lb 15 oz = ☐ oz

    (c) 32 oz = ☐ lb ☐ oz   (d) 69 oz = ☐ lb ☐ oz

11. Add or subtract in compound units.
    (a) 15 lb + 2 lb 3 oz   (b) 12 oz + 12 oz
    (c) 4 lb 13 oz − 9 oz   (d) 4 lb − 9 oz
    (e) 7 lb 5 oz + 14 oz   (f) 6 lb 14 oz + 8 lb 15 oz
    (g) 12 lb − 8 lb 2 oz   (h) 3 lb 1 oz − 1 lb 15 oz

12. A bag of apples has a mass of 800 g.
    What is the mass of 3 such bags?
    Give your answers in kilograms and grams.

13. One bag of sugar has a mass of 900 g.
    What is the mass of 10 such bags of sugar?

14. Emma weighs 59 lb.
    Her mother is 78 lb heavier than she is.
    Find Emma's mother's weight.

15. A bag of carrots weighs 14 oz.
    A bag of lettuce weighs 5 oz less than the bag of carrots.
    What is the weight of the bag of lettuce?

16. David weighs 65 lb.
    John weighs 127 lb.
    Amy weighs 88 lb.
    (a) What is their total weight?
    (b) How much lighter is David than John?

17.

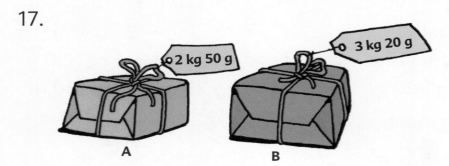

    (a) Find the total mass of the two packages.
    (b) Find the difference in mass between the two packages.

18. A pear has a mass of 280 g.
    An apricot is 60 g lighter than the pear.
    Find the total mass of the pear and the apricot.

19. Sulin has a mass of 34 kg.

    Sally is 8 kg lighter than Sulin.

    What is their total mass?

20. (a) What is the total mass of the 3 sticks
        of butter and the bag of flour?
    (b) If each stick of butter has a mass of 300 g,
        find the mass of the bag of flour in
        kilograms and grams.

21.

    (a) The total mass of the fruit is ▢ g.

    (b) If the apple has a mass of 90 g, find the total mass of
        the two pears.

    (c) If the pears are each the same mass, find the mass of
        each pear.

22. A bag of salt weighs 5 lb.

    A bag of pepper weighs twice as much as a bag of salt.

    What is the total weight of a bag of salt and a bag of pepper?

23. Lily has a mass of 29 kg.

    Her father is 3 times as heavy as she.

    How much heavier is Lily's father than Lily?

24. A tomato weighs 3 oz.

    An avocado weighs 4 oz more
    than the tomato.

    A squash is twice as heavy
    as the avocado.

    What is the weight of the squash?

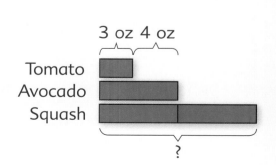

39

25. David has a mass of 39 kg.

    Hugh is twice as heavy as David.

    Matthew's mass is 27 kg less than Hugh's.

    What is Matthew's mass?

26. The total mass of Ali and Sam is 100 kg.

    Ali's mass is 46 kg 500 g. Find Sam's mass.

27. A lobster has a mass of 1 kg 650 g.

    A crab has a mass of 900 g less.

    What is the mass of the crab?

28.

    The total mass of 2 bags of sugar and 1 bag of flour is
    1 kg 900 g.

    If the mass of each bag of sugar is 280 g, find the mass of
    the bag of flour.

29. A box of cherries weighs 1 lb 5 oz.

    A box of peaches weighs 14 oz more than the cherries.

    What is the total weight of the box of
    cherries and the box of peaches?

    305 g − 120 g = 185 g
    We have 185 g of
    potatoes left.

30. Mr. Lin bought 3 kg 5 g of potatoes.

    1 kg 20 g was rotten and he threw them away.

    He told his wife the mass of potatoes left.

    However, she did not believe him.

    How did she know that he was wrong?

    What should be the correct mass?

    Explain your answer.

Review 6, pages 33–36

7 CAPACITY

1 Comparing Capacity

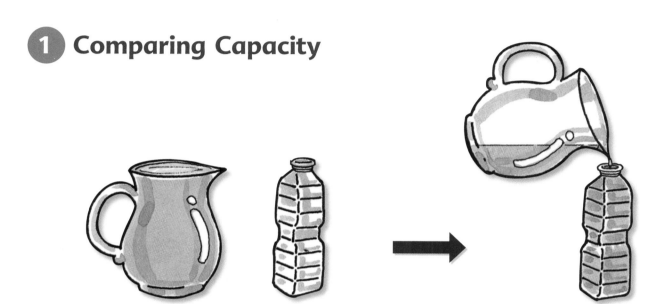

The jug holds more water than the bottle.

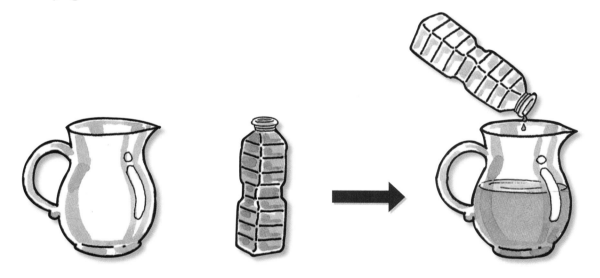

The bottle holds less water than the jug.

1. How many glasses of water does each container hold?

The jug holds ▢ glasses of water.

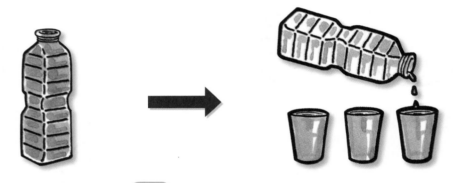

The bottle holds ▢ glasses of water.

2.

A   B   C

Which container holds the most water?
Which container holds the least water?

Exercise 1, pages 37—39

2 Liters

Get a 1-liter beaker and find out how much 1 liter of water is.

We write L for **liter**.

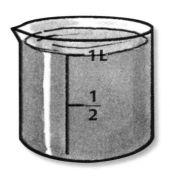

Get some paper cups.
Find out how many paper cups you can fill with 1 liter of water.

1.

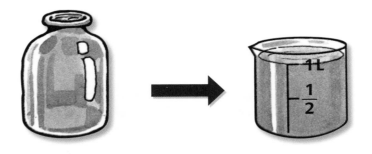

The bottle holds 1 liter of water.

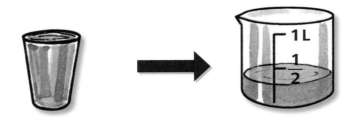

The glass holds less than 1 liter of water.

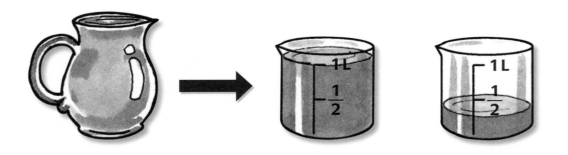

The jug holds more than 1 liter of water.

Which container holds the most water?
Which container holds the least water?

2. Ms. Brown bought a carton of milk.
   How much milk did she buy?

3. These two containers are filled with dishwasher detergent.

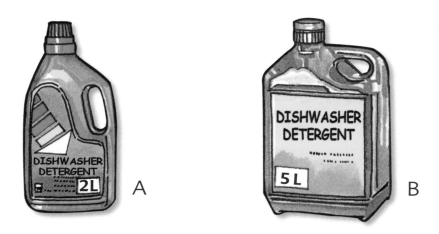

(a) Which container can hold more dishwasher detergent?
(b) How much more?

4. Get a bucket.
   Find out how many liters of
   water the bucket can hold.

5.

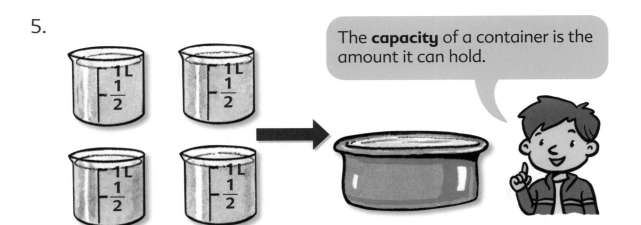

The basin holds 4 liters of water.

The **capacity** of the basin is ⬜ liters.

6. Make a 1-liter bottle.

Get a bottle that can hold 1 L of water.
Pour 1 L of water into it.
Mark the water level.

Use the 1-liter bottle you have made. Estimate and then measure the capacities of some containers.

Exercise 2, page 40

46

3 Liters and Milliliters

We measure capacity in **liters (L)** and **milliliters (ml)**.

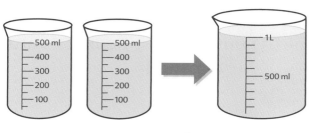

1 L = 1,000 ml

1.

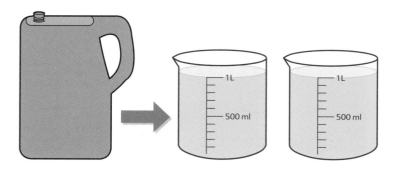

The bottle holds 2 L of water.

Its capacity is ☐ L.

2. (a) Measure 100 ml of water with a
       100-ml beaker.
       Pour the water into a 1-L beaker and note
       where the water level is.

   (b) Repeat (a) until the 1-L beaker contains 1 liter of water.

   (c) 1 L = ⬜ ml

3. Get a teaspoon.
   Find out how many teaspoons of water will make up 10 ml.
   Then find the capacity of the teaspoon.

   The capacity of the teaspoon is about ⬜ ml.

4. Get a paper cup.
   Estimate how many milliliters of water
   the paper cup can hold.
   Then check by measuring the capacity
   of the paper cup.

   The capacity of the paper cup is about ⬜ ml.

5. Complete the sentences.

(a)

The capacity of the mug is ⬜ ml.

(b)

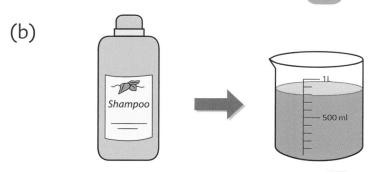

The capacity of the bottle is ⬜ ml.

(c)

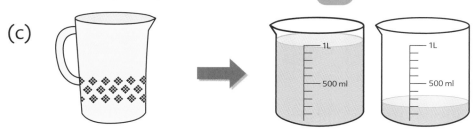

The capacity of the jug is ⬜ L ⬜ ml.

6. What is the total amount of water in each set of beakers?

(a)

(b)

(c)

(d)

Exercise 3, pages 41–44

7. Find the total amount of water in these two beakers.

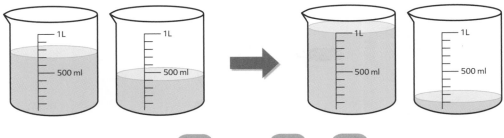

700 ml + 400 ml = ⬜ ml = ⬜ L ⬜ ml

8. Add. Write your answers in liters and milliliters.

   (a) 800 ml + 600 ml   (b) 750 ml + 950 ml

   (c) 535 ml + 875 ml

9. Write 1,500 ml in liters and milliliters.

   1,500 ml = ⬜ L ⬜ ml

10. Write in liters and milliliters.

   (a) 1,200 ml   (b) 2,500 ml   (c) 2,050 ml
   (d) 1,005 ml   (e) 3,400 ml   (f) 3,105 ml

11. (a) Write 2 L in milliliters.

        2 L = ⬜ ml

    (b) Write 2 L 350 ml in milliliters.

        2 L 350 ml = ⬜ ml

12. Write in milliliters.

   (a) 1 L 800 ml   (b) 1 L 80 ml   (c) 1 L 8 ml
   (d) 3 L 25 ml   (e) 2 L 5 ml   (f) 3 L 500 ml

50

13.

Each carton contains 250 ml of milk.
The total amount of milk in 5 cartons is  L ▢ ml.

14.

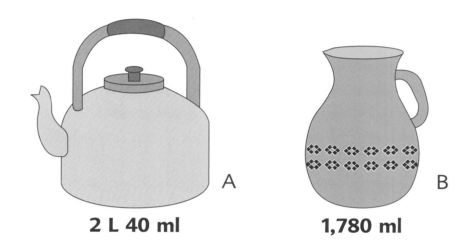

2 L 40 ml   **1,780 ml**

Which container has the greater capacity?
How much greater?

15.

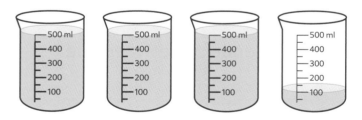

How many milliliters more water
are needed to make up 2 liters?

Exercise 4, pages 45—46

16. Subtract.

(a) 1 L − 320 ml = [ ] ml   (b) 2 L − 320 ml = [ ] ml

(c) 2 L − 1 L 320 ml = [ ] ml   (d) 1 L − 8 ml = [ ] ml

(e) 1 L − 40 ml = [ ] ml   (f) 9 L − 455 ml = [ ] ml

Exercise 5, pages 47—48

17.

1 L 800 ml
A

COOKING OIL

3 L 350 ml
B

(a) Find the total capacity of the two containers.

1 L 800 ml $\xrightarrow{+3 L}$ 4 L 800 ml $\xrightarrow{+350 ml}$ 5 L 150 ml

1 L 800 ml + 3 L 350 ml = [ ] L [ ] ml

The total capacity is [ ] L [ ] ml.

(b) Find the difference in capacity between the two containers.

3 L 350 ml $\xrightarrow{-1 L}$ 2 L 350 ml $\xrightarrow{-800 ml}$ 1 L 550 ml

3 L 350 ml − 1 L 800 ml = [ ] L [ ] ml

The difference in capacity is [ ] L [ ] ml.

52

18. Add or subtract.
    (a) 1 L 500 ml + 500 ml   (b) 2 L 800 ml + 1 L 200 ml
    (c) 3 L 300 ml + 750 ml   (d) 5 L 900 ml + 3 L 240 ml
    (e) 2 L 800 ml − 1 L 780 ml (f) 4 L − 1 L 850 ml
    (g) 4 L 80 ml − 1 L 360 ml   (h) 6 L 5 ml − 2 L 80 ml

Exercise 6, pages 49–50

19. The table shows the capacities of four containers.

Container A	2 L 375 ml
Container B	1 L 750 ml
Container C	1,755 ml
Container D	2,150 ml

    (a) Which container has the greatest capacity?
    (b) Which container has the smallest capacity?
    (c) What is the total capacity of the four containers?

20. Eric bought 20 liters of paint. After painting his house,
    he had 4 liters left. How much paint did he use?

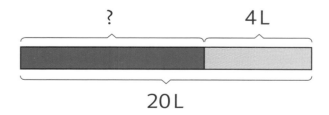

    He used ⬜ liters of paint.

53

21. A tank has a capacity of 30 liters.

    It contains 12 liters of water.
    How many more liters of water are needed to fill the tank?

22. Mr. Ling sold 52 liters of orange juice last week.

    He sold 38 liters of orange juice this week.

    How many liters of orange juice did he sell in the two weeks?

23. Tank A can hold 98 L less water than Tank B.

    Tank B can hold 173 L of water.

    (a) How much water can Tank A hold?

    (b) If the tanks are full, what is the total amount of water
         in both tanks?

24. Mrs. Dale brewed 950 ml of coffee.

    She served 675 ml of coffee to her guests.
    How much coffee did she have left?

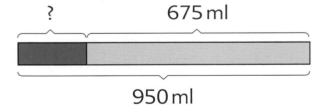

25. Lionel used 520 ml of detergent for his laundry last month.
He used 695 ml of detergent this month.
How much detergent did he use in two months?
Give your answer in liters and milliliters.

26. A flask was filled with 900 ml of water.
Alice poured the water from the flask into a cup.
The cup had a capacity of 250 ml.
How much water was left in the flask?

27. Bottle B has a capacity of 670 ml.
It can hold 180 ml less soda than Bottle A.
(a) What is the capacity of Bottle A?
(b) How much soda is needed to fill both bottles completely?
Leave your answer in liters and millimeters.

28. 6 buckets of water are used to fill up an inflatable pool.
Each bucket holds 8 L of water.
What is the capacity of the inflatable pool?

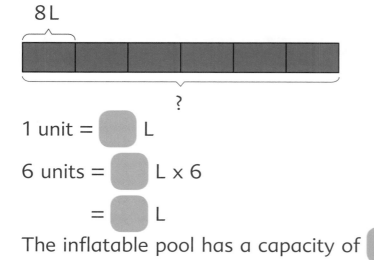

8 L

1 unit = ⬚ L

6 units = ⬚ L x 6

= ⬚ L

The inflatable pool has a capacity of ⬚ L.

29. A fish tank has a capacity of 40 L.
It can hold 8 times as much as a bucket.
What is the capacity of the bucket?

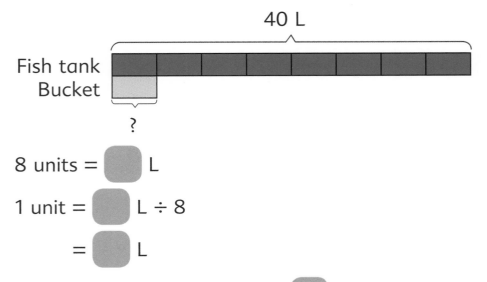

40 L

Fish tank
Bucket

?

8 units = ☐ L

1 unit = ☐ L ÷ 8

= ☐ L

The bucket has a capacity of ☐ L.

30. Davis had 540 ml of hot chocolate.
He poured them equally into 9 cups.
How much hot chocolate was there
in each cup?

540 = 54 tens

?

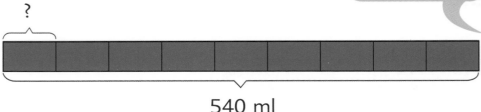

540 ml

9 units = ☐ ml

1 unit = ☐ ml ÷ 9

= ☐ ml

There were ☐ ml of hot chocolate in each cup.

31. Amelia bought 3 bottles of soft drinks.
    Each bottle contains 550 ml of liquid.
    How much soft drinks did Amelia buy altogether?

32. A tank has a capacity of 49 L.
    A bucket has a capacity of 7 L.
    How many times will the bucket need to be filled and poured into the tank to fill it completely?

33. Mrs. Morris drinks 400 ml of milk a day.
    How much milk does she drink in a week?
    Leave your answers in milliliters.

34. The total capacity of 4 cartons of apple juice is 4,800 ml.
    Find the capacity of 1 carton of apple juice.

35. The volume of a bottle of juice is 875 ml.
    What is the volume of 6 bottles?
    Leave your answer in liters and milliliters.

Exercises 7, pages 51–53

4 Gallons, Quarts, Pints, and Cups

The capacity of a container can also be measured in cups, pints, quarts, and gallons.

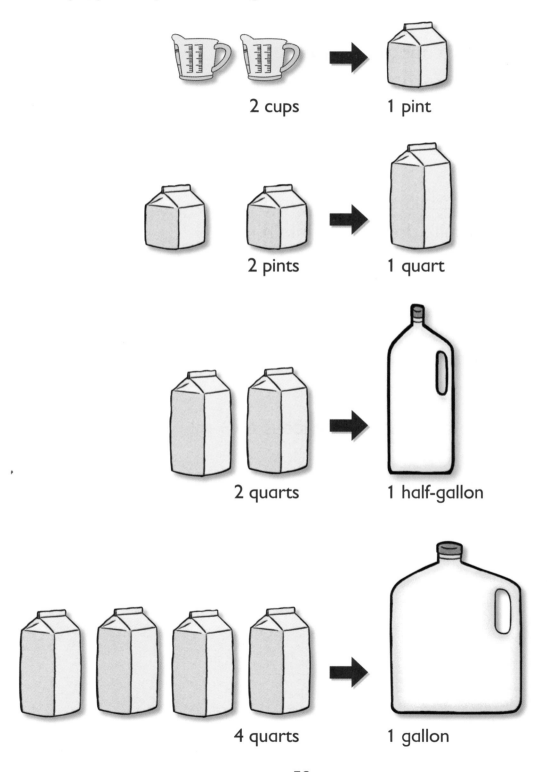

2 cups → 1 pint

2 pints → 1 quart

2 quarts → 1 half-gallon

4 quarts → 1 gallon

We write **c** for **cup**.
We write **pt** for **pint**.
We write **qt** for **quart**.
We write **gal** for **gallon**.

1. Fill a 1-gal milk carton with water.
   Find out how many cups you can fill with 1 gal of water.

2. Compare a quart to a liter.

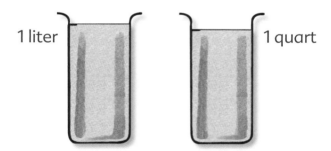

1 quart of water is slightly less than 1 liter of water.

3. Compare a cup to a milliliter.
   About how many milliliters are there in a cup?

4.   **CUP   PINT   QUART   GALLON**

Which of the above units of measure would you most likely use to measure:

(a) the amount of water in a fish tank?

(b) the amount of milk you drink daily?

(c) a carton of heavy whipping cream?

(d) a carton of fruit juice?

5. (a) How many quarts of milk are there in 1 gallon of milk?

(1 qt)(1 qt)(1 qt)(1 qt) 1 gallon

There are ▢ quarts in 1 gallon.

(b) How many quarts of milk are there in 5 gallons of milk?

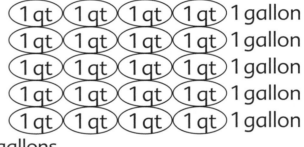

$5 \times 4 =$ ▢

There are ▢ quarts in 5 gallons.

6. Jamie pours 32 quarts of cider into gallon jugs. How many gallon jugs does she need?

$32 \div 4 =$ ▢

She needs ▢ gallon jugs.

7. Tina buys 3 quarts of apple juice and pours the apple juice into pint jugs. How many pint jugs does she use?

$3 \times 2 =$ ▢

She uses ▢ pint jugs.

8. Fill in the missing numbers.

   (a) 1 qt = ☐ c   (b) 1 gal = ☐ c

   3 qt = ☐ c   3 gal = ☐ c

   3 qt 3 c = ☐ c   3 gal 1 qt = ☐ c

9. A recipe for 6 popovers calls for 1 cup of milk.
   Mitch has 3 baking trays that each hold
   12 popovers.
   He wants to use all 3 trays.

   (a) How many cups of milk does he need?

   Mitch needs ☐ c of milk for 12 popovers.

   He needs ☐ c of milk for 3 trays.

   (b) He buys 2 qt of milk.
   How many cups of milk will he have left over after
   he makes the popovers?

   He will have ☐ c of milk left over.

10. Write 15 pt in quarts and pints.

    15 pt = ☐ qt ☐ pt

2 pt = 1 qt
15 ÷ 2 = 7 with a
remainder of 1.

11. Find the missing numbers.

    (a) 21 c = ☐ pt ☐ c   (b) 14 qt = ☐ gal ☐ qt
    (c) 19 c = ☐ qt ☐ c   (d) 28 pt = ☐ gal ☐ pt

Exercise 9, pages 56—57

12.

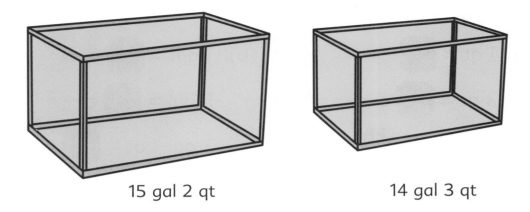

15 gal 2 qt   14 gal 3 qt

(a) What is the total capacity of the two fish tanks?

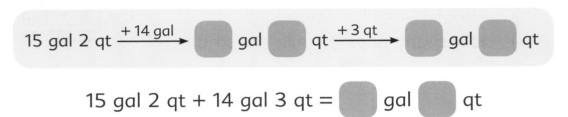

15 gal 2 qt $\xrightarrow{+\,14\,gal}$ ⬜ gal ⬜ qt $\xrightarrow{+\,3\,qt}$ ⬜ gal ⬜ qt

15 gal 2 qt + 14 gal 3 qt = ⬜ gal ⬜ qt

(b) What is the difference in the capacity of the two fish tanks?

15 gal 2 qt $\xrightarrow{-\,14\,gal}$ ⬜ gal ⬜ qt $\xrightarrow{-\,3\,qt}$ ⬜ gal ⬜ qt

15 gal 2 qt − 14 gal 3 qt = ⬜ gal ⬜ qt

13. Add or subtract.

(a) 12 gal 3 qt + 9 gal 3 qt = ⬜ gal ⬜ qt

(b) 10 gal 1 qt − 8 gal 3 qt = ⬜ gal ⬜ qt

(c) 36 qt − 15 qt 3 c = ⬜ qt ⬜ c

Exercise 10, page 58

1. What is the volume of the water in the beaker?

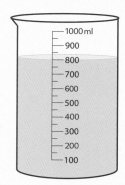

    (A) 600 ml (B) 750 ml (C) 800 ml   (D) 875 ml

2. Write 5 L 8 ml in milliliters.
    (A) 508 ml (B) 580 ml (C) 5,008 ml (D) 5,800 ml

3. How many quarts are there in 1 gallon?
    (A) 2   (B) 4   (C) 8   (D) 16

4. How many pints are needed to fill a 6-gallon tank?
    (A) 12   (B) 24   (C) 48   (D) 96

5. Mr. Clifford needs 6 cups to fill a jug.

    He needs 4 jugs to fill a container.

    How many cups does he need altogether?
    (A) 8   (B) 10   (C) 12   (D) 24

6. Select True or False.
    (a) 1 L 250 ml > 2 L 9 ml   True / False
    (b) 650 ml + 950 ml = 600 ml + 1 L   True / False

7. Select True or False.
    (a) 1 quart < 2 pints   True / False
    (b) 2 gallons < 30 cups   True / False

8. Write in milliliters.
   (a) 3 L
   (b) 1 L 200 ml
   (c) 2 L 55 ml
   (d) 2 L 650 ml
   (e) 3 L 65 ml
   (f) 4 L 5 ml

9. Write in liters and milliliters.
   (a) 5,000 ml
   (b) 1,600 ml
   (c) 2,250 ml
   (d) 3,205 ml
   (e) 2,074 ml
   (f) 1,009 ml

10. Write in cups.
    (a) 8 pt
    (b) 15 pt 1 c
    (c) 2 qt
    (d) 5 qt 3 c
    (e) 3 gal
    (f) 7 gal 2 qt

11. Write in pints.
    (a) 7 qt
    (b) 11 qt 1 pt
    (c) 3 gal
    (d) 4 gal 3 pt
    (e) 8 gal 2 qt
    (f) 10 gal 2 c

12. Write in quarts.
    (a) 10 gal
    (b) 23 gal 1 qt
    (c) 4 gal 4 pt

13. Fill in the blanks.
    (a) 19 pt = ☐ qt ☐ pt
    (b) 25 c = ☐ qt ☐ c
    (c) 31 c = ☐ pt ☐ c
    (d) 33 c = ☐ gal ☐ c
    (e) 34 qt = ☐ gal ☐ qt
    (f) 26 pt = ☐ gal ☐ pt

14. Which sign goes in the ◯, >, < or =?
    (a) 1 L ◯ 980 ml
    (b) 2 L 50 ml ◯ 2,050 ml
    (c) 4 L 8 ml ◯ 4,800 ml
    (d) 5 gal 1 qt ◯ 12 qt
    (e) 12 qt 1 pt ◯ 23 pt
    (f) 15 c ◯ 7 pt 1 c

15. Add or subtract.
    (a) 4 L 450 ml + 2 L 350 ml
    (b) 9 L 800 ml + 7 L 300 ml
    (c) 10 L − 2 L 150 ml
    (d) 5 L 700 ml − 1 L 490 ml
    (e) 6 L 40 ml − 1 L 620 ml
    (f) 8 L 5 ml − 3 L 20 ml

16. Add or subtract.

    (a) 3 qt 1 c + 7 qt 1 c = ☐ qt ☐ c

    (b) 12 gal − 7 gal 1 qt = ☐ gal ☐ qt

    (c) 258 pt − 185 pt 1 c = ☐ pt ☐ c

17. A class drank 18 L of fruit punch at a party.
    12 L of fruit punch was left.
    How much fruit punch was there at first?

18. A water tank can hold 250 liters of water.
    It has 185 liters of water in it now.
    How many more liters of water are needed to fill the tank?

19. The capacity of a container is 24 liters.
    How many buckets of water are needed to fill up the
    container if the capacity of the bucket is 3 liters?

20. Ms. Chavez fills a container with 9 cartons of orange juice.
    Each carton contains 2 liters of orange juice.
    What is the capacity of the container?

21. Bucket A holds 12 liters of water.
    Bucket B holds 8 liters of water.

    (a) Which bucket holds
    more water?
    (b) How much more?

22. A tub contains 1 liter of yogurt.
    Peter eats 325 ml of it.
    How much yogurt is left?

23. A large jug contains 14 cups of juice.
    The juice is poured into bottles.
    Each bottle has a capacity of 3 cups.
    What is the fewest number of bottles needed for all the juice?

24. Peter used 128 gal of gas last month.
    He used 25 gal more gas this month.
    How much gas did he use this month?

25. A tank can hold 115 gal of water.
    It contains 38 gal of water.
    How many more gallons of water can be poured into this tank?

26. Morgan drinks 2 c of milk daily.
    How many pints of milk does she drink in a week?

27. A store sold 302 qt of milk last month.
    It sold 29 qt less milk this month.
    How much milk did the store sell this month?

28. The capacity of a kettle is 2 qt.
    There is 1 pt of water in the kettle now.
    How many more pints of water are needed to fill the kettle?

29. Ms. Perez bought a gallon of milk.
    She drank 3 quarts of it by the end of the week.
    How many quarts of milk were left in the jug?

30. Container A holds 13 gal of water.
    Container B holds 7 gal 1 qt less water than Container A.
    How much water does Container B hold?

31. The table shows the amount of milk
    3 children drank in a week.

    | Ben | 6 quarts |
    | Emma | 4 quarts |
    | Carlos | 2 quarts |

    (a) Find the total number of quarts
        of milk they drank in a week.
    (b) What is the total number of cups of milk they
        drank in a week?
    (c) What is the total number of gallons of milk they
        drank in a week?

32. The capacity of a container is 8 L.
    It contains 4 L 650 ml of water.
    How much more water is needed to fill the container?

33. Container X holds 2 L 800 ml of water.
    Container Y holds 1 L 600 ml more water than Container X.
    How much water does Container Y hold?

34.

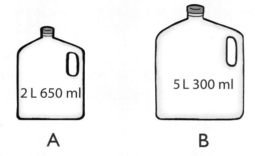

A   B

    The capacity of Container A is 2 L 650 ml.
    The capacity of Container B is 5 L 300 ml.
    (a) What is the total capacity of the two containers?
    (b) How much more water can Container B hold than
         Container A?

35. Adam bought 6 cans of paint.
    Each can contained 3 L of paint.
    He had 2 L 400 ml of paint left after painting his house.
    (a) How much paint did he buy?
    (b) How much paint did he use?

36. Mrs. Stevens drinks 50 gal of water in 100 days.
    How many cups of water does she drink each day?
    Explain your answer.

Review 7, pages 59–62

8 MONEY

1 Dollars and Cents

Read the prices of these items.
Fill in the missing numbers.

$35.25

$35   25¢

The dot (·) separates the cents from the dollars.

$35.25 = dollars cents

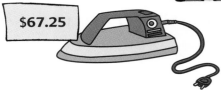

$67.25 = dollars cents

$75.40 = dollars cents

$32.75 = dollars cents

1. How much money is there in each set?

   (a)
   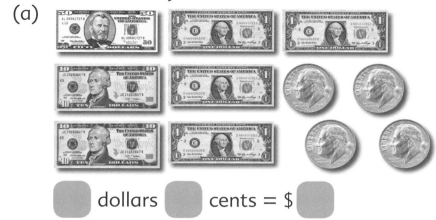

   ⬜ dollars ⬜ cents = $ ⬜

   (b)

   ⬜ dollars ⬜ cents = $ ⬜

2. (a) Write $1.25 in cents.

   $1.25 = ⬜ ¢

   $1 = 100¢

   (b) Write 170¢ in dollars and cents.

   170¢ = $ ⬜

3. Write in cents.

   (a) $0.30
   (b) $1.95
   (c) $4.05

4. Write in dollars and cents.

   (a) 85¢
   (b) 160¢
   (c) 345¢

5. How much more money is needed to make $1?

   (a) $0.70 + \$\boxed{} = \$1$

   (b) $0.55 + \$\boxed{} = \$1$

   (c) $25¢ + \boxed{} = \$1$

   (d) $40¢ + \boxed{} = \$1$

6. How much money is there?

   (a)

   6 quarters = $\$\boxed{}$

   (b)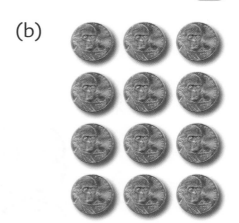

   12 nickels = $\$\boxed{}$

   (c) Lily has 6 quarters and 12 nickels.
   How much money does she have altogether?

7. There are 4 nickels, 2 quarters, and 4 one-dollar bills in a purse.
   What is the total amount of money in the purse?

Exercise 1, pages 63–64

70

② Addition

Morgan bought a box of plums for $13.25 and a cake for $6.50.
How much did she spend altogether?

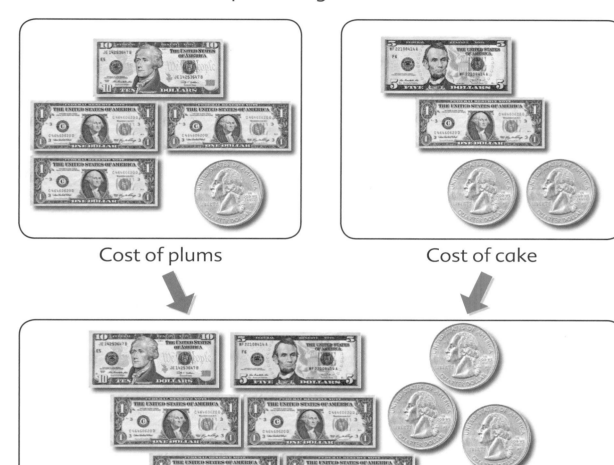

Cost of plums

Cost of cake

Total cost of plums and cake

$13.25 + $6.50 = $

She spent $ [ ] altogether.

1. Find the value of
   (a) $1.50 + 20¢   (b) $14.20 + 65¢   (c) $38.40 + 35¢
   (d) $2.75 + 25¢   (e) $25.40 + 60¢   (f) $33.85 + 15¢

2. Complete the equations.

   (a) $2.85 + 20¢ = $ ▢

   (b) $2.70 + 60¢ = $ ▢

   (c) $5.65 + 45¢ = $ ▢

   (d) $16.95 + 45¢ = $ ▢

   (e) $24.70 + 95¢ = $ ▢

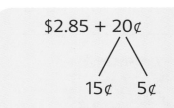

$2.85 + 20¢

15¢   5¢

85¢ and 15¢ make $1.

3. Complete the equations.

   (a) $25.70 $\xrightarrow{+ \$4}$ $ ▢ $\xrightarrow{+ 10¢}$ $ ▢

   $25.70 + $4.10 = $ ▢

   (b) $34.65 $\xrightarrow{+ \$2}$ $ ▢ $\xrightarrow{+ 35¢}$ $ ▢

   $34.65 + $2.35 = $ ▢

   (c) $30.80 $\xrightarrow{+ \$5}$ $ ▢ $\xrightarrow{+ 40¢}$ $ ▢

   $30.80 + $5.40 = $ ▢

   (d) $24.70 $\xrightarrow{+ \$10}$ $ ▢ $\xrightarrow{+ 50¢}$ $ ▢

   $24.70 + $10.50 = $ ▢

4. Find the value of
   (a) $14.65 + $6.20   (b) $13.60 + $24.40
   (c) $32.70 + $24.50   (d) $15.60 + $23.70
   (e) $40.85 + $19.65   (f) $28.35 + $26.75

5. We can add $24.55 and $13.65 like this:

```
  $24.55
+ $13.65
  $38.20
```

```
    ¹ ¹
  2,455
+ 1,365
  3,820
```

Use this method to find the value of the following.

(a) $35.32 + $21.68

(b) $27.71 + $13.90

(c) $46.70 + $36.63

(d) $56.85 + $16.38

(e) $28.66 + $32.49

(f) $36.92 + $24.85

Exercise 2, pages 65—67

6. Ali bought a toy car for $6.95.
   He also spent $2.80 on a meal.
   How much money did he spend altogether?

$2.80 + $6.95 = $ [ ]

He spent $ [ ] altogether.

7. Miguel paid $11.90 for a pen.
   He had $24.65 left.
   How much money did he have at first?

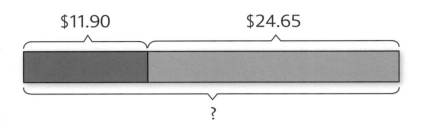

$11.90 + $24.65 = $ ◻

He had $ ◻ at first.

8. John saves $6.75 this week.
   He saves $2.35 less this week than last week.
   How much money did he save last week?

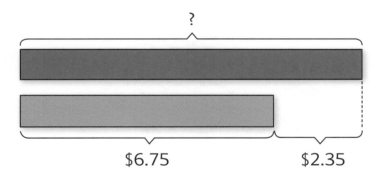

$6.75 + $2.35 = $ ◻

He saved $ ◻ last week.

9. Adam bought a toothbrush and a tube of toothpaste.
   The toothbrush cost $6.50.
   The tube of toothpaste cost $1.80.
   How much did he pay altogether?

10. A toy car costs $16.80.
    A toy airplane costs $5.60 more than the toy car.
    What is the cost of the toy airplane?

11. After spending $24.60, Holly had $75.40 left.
    How much money did she have at first?

12. Mrs. White sold some clothes for $42.50.
    She sold some shoes for $51.85.
    How much did she earn altogether?

Exercise 3, pages 68—69

③ Subtraction

Chris bought a music CD and a video game for $56.50.
The CD cost $25.30.
How much did the video game cost?

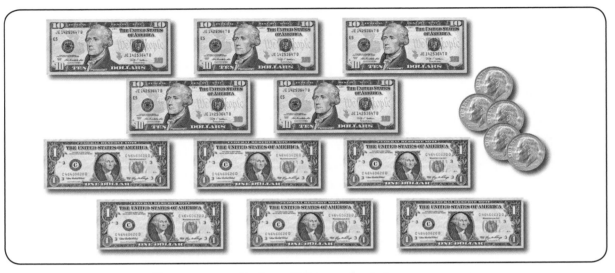

The cost of the CD and video game

The cost of the CD

The cost of the video game

$56.50 − $25.30 = $ ▢

The video game cost $ ▢ .

1. Find the value of
   (a) $2.60 − 20¢
   (b) $8.75 − 30¢
   (c) $35.85 − 45¢
   (d) $1.50 − 25¢
   (e) $6.50 − 45¢
   (f) $46.70 − 25¢

2. Complete the equations.
   (a) $1 − 60¢ = ☐ ¢
   (b) $1.30 − 60¢ = ☐ ¢
   (c) $1.25 − 35¢ = ☐ ¢
   (d) $1.40 − 85¢ = ☐ ¢

3. Complete the equations.
   (a) $3.20 − 80¢ = $☐
   (b) $14.65 − 90¢ = $☐
   (c) $46.25 − 45¢ = $☐
   (d) $32.05 − 85¢ = $☐

   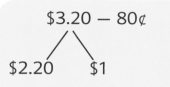

   $3.20 − 80¢

   $2.20 $1

   Subtract 80¢ from $1.

4. Complete the equations.
   (a) $16.80 $\xrightarrow{-\$4}$ $☐ $\xrightarrow{-60¢}$ $☐
       $16.80 − $4.60 = $☐
   (b) $37.70 $\xrightarrow{-\$10}$ $☐ $\xrightarrow{-20¢}$ $☐
       $37.70 − $10.20 = $☐
   (c) $29.20 $\xrightarrow{-\$12}$ $☐ $\xrightarrow{-50¢}$ $☐
       $29.20 − $12.50 = $☐

5. Find the value of
   (a) $47.50 − $12
   (b) $35.70 − $0.85
   (c) $58 − $12.60
   (d) $64.40 − $11.60
   (e) $25.05 − $15.35
   (f) $56.20 − $28.95

6. Find the value of
   (a) $10 − $4.70   (b) $30 − $7.20   (c) $50 − $8.25
   (d) $50 − $23.80   (e) $100 − $52.90 (f) $100 − $39.45

7. We can subtract $23.70 from $46.20 like this:

$$
\begin{array}{r}
\$46.20 \\
- \ \$23.70 \\
\hline
\$22.50
\end{array}
$$

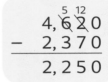

   Use this method to find the value of
   (a) $45.12 − $23.45
   (b) $36.35 − $10.87
   (c) $94.06 − $37.82
   (d) $52.23 − $35.75
   (e) $70.21 − $28.74
   (f) $65.05 − $35.87

Exercise 4, pages 70–72

8. Nancy bought a tin of cookies that cost $5.65.
   She gave the cashier $10.
   How much change did she receive?

   $10 − $5.65 = $ ⬜

   She received $ ⬜ change.

9. Mei had $20.
   She bought an umbrella and had $14.60 left.
   What was the cost of the umbrella?

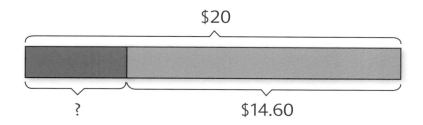

$20 − $14.60 = $ ☐

The umbrella cost $ ☐ .

10. Jim has $25.50.
    He wants to buy a watch that costs $35.
    How much more money does he need?

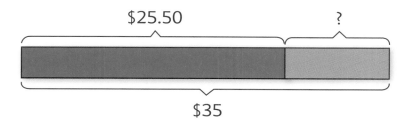

$35 − $25.50 = $ ☐

He needs $ ☐ more.

11. Sean had $10.
    After paying for his lunch, he had $3.59 left.
    How much did his lunch cost?

12. Anne had $40.50.
    She bought a pen for $6.80 and a book for $13.20.
    How much money did she have left?

13. A skirt costs $42.50.
    A shirt costs $16.89.
    How much more does the skirt cost than the shirt?

14. A badminton racket costs $15.90.
    A tennis racket costs $53.50.
    How much cheaper is the badminton racket than the
    tennis racket?

15. Jerome wants to buy a fishing rod which costs $62.50.
    He only has $48.60.
    How much more money does he need?

Exercise 5, pages 73–74

1. Which amount is the greatest?
   (A) 25 dimes   (B) 80 nickels
   (C) 2 dollars   (D) 10 quarters

2. Fourteen dollars and seven cents is the same as _____.
   (A) $14.07   (B) $14.70
   (C) $40.07   (D) $40.70

3. 1,050¢ = _____
   (A) $10.05   (B) $10.50
   (C) $105.00   (D) $100.50

4. Livia received $30 from her father to buy a gift for her brother.
   The gift she bought cost $21.85.
   How much change did Livia receive after paying for the gift?
   (A) $8.15   (B) $9.15
   (C) $11.15   (D) $18.15

5. Select True or False.
   (a) $1 = 1,000¢   True / False
   (b) 245¢ + 475¢ > 700¢   True / False

6. Select True or False.
   (a) $83 < $81.25 + $0.85   True / False
   (b) $47.45 + $0.95 = $47.45 + $1 − $0.05   True / False

7. Write each amount of money in words.
   (a) $1.48   (b) $30.60
   (c) $35.75   (d) $94.05

8. (a) How many $10 bills can you get for $200?
    (b) How many quarters can you get for $2?
    (c) How many dimes can you get for $3?
    (d) How many nickels can you get for $1.50?

9. Write in cents.
    (a) $0.20   (b) $0.65   (c) $7.00   (d) $2.05
    (e) $5.60   (f) $3.95   (g) $8.08   (h) $9.99

10. Write in dollars and cents.
    (a) 5¢   (b) 60¢   (c) 400¢   (d) 210¢
    (e) 855¢   (f) 305¢   (g) 625¢   (h) 1,000¢

11. Find the missing amount of money in each of the following:
    (a) 30¢ + ☐ = $1   (b) ☐ + 45¢ = $1

    (c) $0.40 + ☐ = $1   (d) ☐ + $0.65 = $1

12. Add or subtract.
    (a) $26.20 + $13.50   (b) $39.45 + $60.55
    (c) $36.70 − $15.35   (d) $60.50 − $24.45
    (e) $48.40 + $27.30   (f) $15.95 + $24.35
    (g) $52.30 − $30.70   (h) $40.05 − $16.30
    (i) $65.96 + $25.78   (j) $36.92 + $54.55
    (k) $72.20 − $26.83   (l) $81.00 − $31.85
    (m) $34.45 + $28.95   (n) $32.05 − $22.95
    (o) $72.95 + $26.95   (p) $64.25 − $35.95

13. Juanita spent $4.80 on strings and $2.50 on beads to make a
    flowerpot hanger.

    How much did it cost her to make a flowerpot hanger?

14. The usual price of a CD player is $43.
    Its sale price is $29.95.
    How much less is the sale price than the usual price?

15. A sweater and a pair of jeans cost $98.00.
    The pair of jeans costs $75.95.
    How much more does the pair of jeans cost than the sweater?

16. Ms. Greene bought some vegetables for $2.40 and a fish
    for $3.70.
    She had $21.30 left.
    How much money did she have at first?

17. Vinod saved $33.50 last week.
    He saved $48.50 this week.
    His target was to save $100.
    How much more did he need to save to meet his target?

18. Jeremy bought a camera case for $28.25.
    He gave the storekeeper $50.00.
    The storekeeper did some calculations on paper and returned
    Jeremy $28.25.
    Jeremy looked at the calculations and realized the mistake that
    the storekeeper made.

$$
\begin{array}{r}
\$ \quad \ ^4\!5 \ \ ^1\!0 \\
-\$ \ 2 \quad 8\ .\ 2\ \ 5 \\
\hline
\$ \ 2 \quad 8\ .\ 2\ \ 5 \\
\end{array}
$$

What was the storekeeper's mistake?
Explain your answer.

Review 8, pages 77–82

9 FRACTIONS

1 Fraction of a Whole

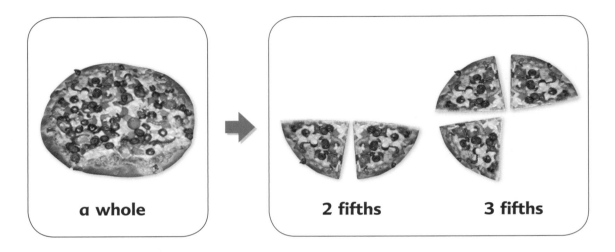

a whole   2 fifths   3 fifths

How many fifths are there in a whole?

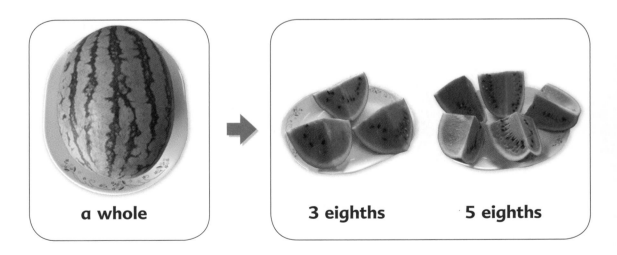

a whole   3 eighths   5 eighths

How many eighths are there in a whole?

1. Fill in the blanks.

(a) $\frac{2}{5}$ of the bar is shaded.

$\frac{2}{5}$ is ⬜ out of the ⬜ equal parts.

$\frac{1}{5} + \frac{1}{5} = \frac{2}{5} =$ ⬜ fifths

(b) $\frac{3}{5}$ of the bar is **not** shaded.

$\frac{3}{5}$ is ⬜ out of the ⬜ equal parts.

$\frac{1}{5} + \frac{1}{5} + \frac{1}{5} = \frac{3}{5} =$ ⬜ fifths

(c) 1 whole = ⬜ fifths

$\frac{1}{5} + \frac{1}{5} + \frac{1}{5} + \frac{1}{5} + \frac{1}{5} = \frac{\boxed{}}{5} = 1$

2. Fill in the blanks.

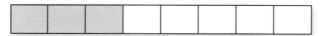

(a) $\frac{3}{8}$ of the bar is shaded.

⬜ of the bar is **not** shaded.

(b) 1 whole = ⬜ eighths

$1 = \frac{\boxed{}}{8}$

(c) $\frac{3}{8}$ and ⬜ make 1 whole.

85

3. What fraction of each shape is shaded?
   What fraction is not shaded?

(a)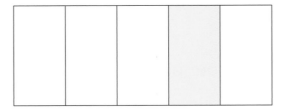

(b)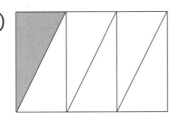

(c)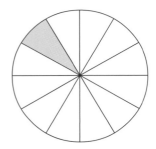

(d)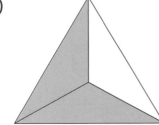

(e)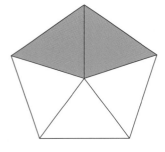

(f)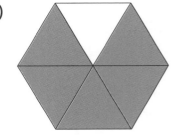

(g)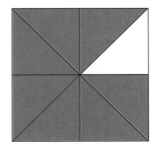

(h)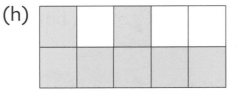

Exercise 1, pages 83—88

86

4.

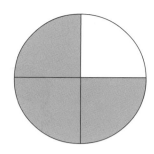

$$\frac{3}{4} \leftarrow \textbf{numerator}$$
$$\leftarrow \textbf{denominator}$$

In the fraction $\frac{3}{4}$, 3 is the numerator and 4 is the denominator.

Name the numerator and denominator of each of these fractions.

(a) $\frac{2}{5}$ (b) $\frac{4}{10}$ (c) $\frac{6}{7}$ (d) $\frac{6}{9}$

5. Which fraction of the circle is greater, $\frac{1}{5}$ or $\frac{1}{3}$?

   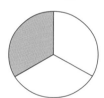

6. Which fraction of the circle is greater, $\frac{3}{4}$ or $\frac{3}{5}$?

7. Which fraction of the bar is greater, $\frac{3}{8}$ or $\frac{5}{8}$?

8.

 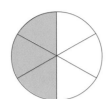 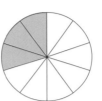

The fractions $\frac{3}{5}$, $\frac{3}{6}$, and $\frac{3}{10}$ have a common numerator.

 is the smallest fraction.　　　 is the greatest fraction.

9.

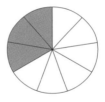 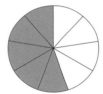 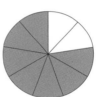

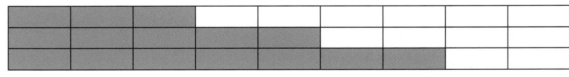

The fractions $\frac{3}{9}$, $\frac{5}{9}$, and $\frac{7}{9}$ have a common denominator.

　　　 is the smallest fraction.　　　 is the greatest fraction.

10. Each set of fractions is for the same whole.
Arrange the fractions in order.
Begin with the smallest.

(a) $\frac{1}{5}$, $\frac{1}{7}$, $\frac{1}{3}$

(b) $\frac{2}{7}$, $\frac{2}{3}$, $\frac{2}{9}$

(c) $\frac{5}{8}$, $\frac{7}{8}$, $\frac{4}{8}$

(d) $\frac{5}{12}$, $\frac{9}{12}$, $\frac{4}{12}$

11. Fill in the blank.

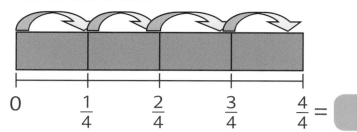

$$\frac{4}{4} = \boxed{}$$

The number line has 4 equal parts. Each part represent $\frac{1}{4}$.

$\frac{1}{4} + \frac{1}{4} + \frac{1}{4} + \frac{1}{4} = \frac{4}{4}$

$\frac{4}{4}$ is also 1 whole.

12. Complete the number line.

(a)
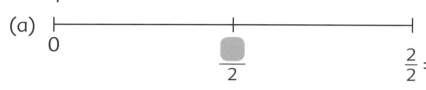

$$\frac{2}{2} = \boxed{}$$

(b)

$$\frac{5}{\boxed{}} = \boxed{}$$

(c)

$$\frac{6}{6} = \boxed{}$$

(d)

$$\frac{7}{7} = \boxed{}$$

(e)
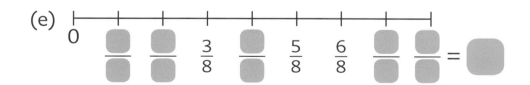

$$\frac{\boxed{}}{\boxed{}} = \boxed{}$$

(f)
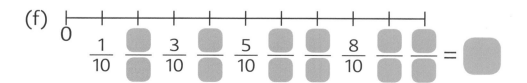

$$\boxed{} = \boxed{}$$

13. Rod A is $\frac{4}{5}$ m long, Rod B is $\frac{1}{5}$ m long, and Rod C is $\frac{2}{5}$ m long.

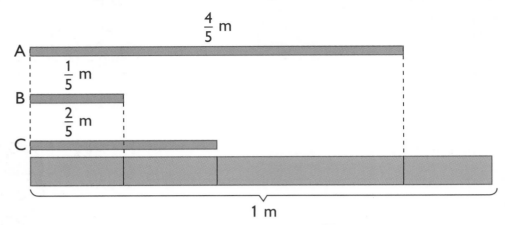

(a) Rod ⬜ is the longest. It is $\frac{\square}{5}$ m longer than Rod C.

(b) Rod B and Rod C together are ⬜ m long.

(c) There are 5 rods the same length as Rod B.
    How long would they be if placed end to end?

14. Each meter has been divided into equal parts.
    What fraction does each letter represent?

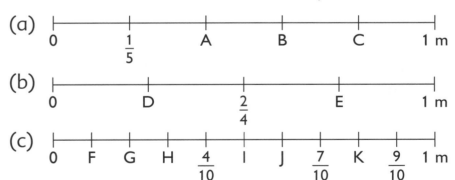

15. Which sign goes in the ⬤ , >, <, or = ?

(a) $\frac{3}{5}$ m ⬤ $\frac{3}{4}$ m   (b) $\frac{5}{5}$ cm ⬤ 1 cm

(c) $\frac{3}{10}$ m ⬤ $\frac{5}{10}$ m   (d) $\frac{1}{4}$ in. ⬤ $\frac{1}{8}$ in.

Exercise 2, pages 89–93

2 Equivalent Fractions

Fold a piece of paper into 2 equal parts.
Shade 1 part.

$\frac{1}{2}$ of the paper is shaded.

Fold the paper again.

1 out of
2 equal parts

$\frac{2}{4}$ of the paper is shaded.

Fold the paper again.

2 out of
4 equal parts

$\frac{4}{8}$ of the paper is shaded.

4 out of
8 equal parts

The fractions $\frac{1}{2}$, $\frac{2}{4}$, and $\frac{4}{8}$ have different numerators
and denominators.
But they are equal.

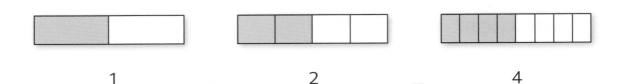

$$\frac{1}{2} \qquad = \qquad \frac{2}{4} \qquad = \qquad \frac{4}{8}$$

$\frac{1}{2}$, $\frac{2}{4}$, and $\frac{4}{8}$ are **equivalent fractions**.

Name some more equivalent fractions of $\frac{1}{2}$.

$\frac{2}{4}$ and $\frac{4}{8}$ are different ways of writing $\frac{1}{2}$.

1.

$\frac{2}{3}$ of the bar is shaded.

What are the missing numerators?

(a) $\frac{2}{3} = \frac{\blacksquare}{6}$

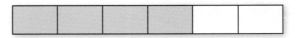

(b) $\frac{2}{3} = \frac{\blacksquare}{9}$

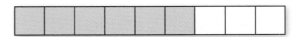

(c) $\frac{2}{3} = \frac{\blacksquare}{12}$

2. What are the missing numerators and denominators?

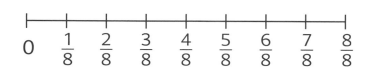

$\frac{3}{4}$ and $\frac{6}{8}$ are equivalent fractions.

(a) $\frac{3}{4} = \frac{\square}{8}$

0	$\frac{1}{8}$	$\frac{2}{8}$	$\frac{3}{8}$	$\frac{4}{8}$	$\frac{5}{8}$	$\frac{6}{8}$	$\frac{7}{8}$	$\frac{8}{8}$

(b) $\frac{1}{4} = \frac{2}{\square}$

0	$\frac{1}{4}$	$\frac{2}{4}$	$\frac{3}{4}$	$\frac{4}{4}$

(c) $\frac{1}{2} = \frac{\square}{4} = \frac{3}{\square} = \frac{\square}{8}$

0	$\frac{1}{2}$	$\frac{2}{2}$

(d) $\frac{2}{3} = \frac{\square}{6}$

0	$\frac{1}{6}$	$\frac{2}{6}$	$\frac{3}{6}$	$\frac{4}{6}$	$\frac{5}{6}$	$\frac{6}{6}$

(e) $\frac{1}{3} = \frac{\square}{\square}$

0	$\frac{1}{3}$	$\frac{2}{3}$	$\frac{3}{3}$

$\frac{?}{8} = \frac{?}{6} = \frac{?}{4} = \frac{?}{2} = 1$

3. The line is $\frac{3}{4}$ in. long.
Name some equivalent fractions for $\frac{3}{4}$ in.

$\frac{3}{4}$ in. $= \frac{6}{\square}$ in. $= \frac{12}{\square}$ in.

Exercise 3, pages 94–96

93

4. What are the missing numerators and denominators?

(a)

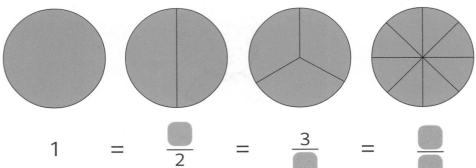

$$1 \quad = \quad \frac{\boxed{}}{2} \quad = \quad \frac{3}{\boxed{}} \quad = \quad \frac{\boxed{}}{\boxed{}}$$

(b)

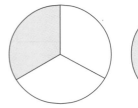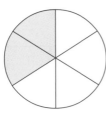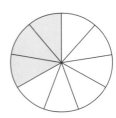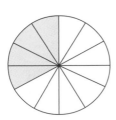

$$\frac{1}{3} \quad = \quad \frac{\boxed{}}{6} \quad = \quad \frac{3}{\boxed{}} \quad = \quad \frac{\boxed{}}{\boxed{}}$$

To find an equivalent fraction, multiply the numerator and denominator by the same number.

$$\overset{\times 2}{\frac{1}{3} = \frac{\boxed{}}{6}}_{\times 2} \qquad \overset{\times 3}{\frac{1}{3} = \frac{3}{\boxed{}}}_{\times 3}$$

5. Find the missing numerator or denominator.

(a) $\dfrac{1}{4} = \dfrac{\boxed{}}{12}$

(b) $\dfrac{2}{3} = \dfrac{\boxed{}}{9}$

(c) $\dfrac{1}{5} = \dfrac{\boxed{}}{10}$

(d) $\dfrac{1}{6} = \dfrac{3}{\boxed{}}$

(e) $\dfrac{3}{5} = \dfrac{6}{\boxed{}}$

(f) $\dfrac{3}{4} = \dfrac{6}{\boxed{}}$

Exercise 4, pages 97—98

6. What are the missing numerators and denominators?

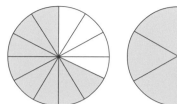 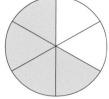 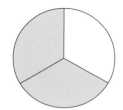

$$\frac{8}{12} \quad = \quad \frac{\boxed{}}{6} \quad = \quad \frac{2}{\boxed{}}$$

To find an equivalent fraction, divide the numerator and denominator by the same number.

$$\overset{\div 2}{\frac{8}{12}} = \frac{\boxed{}}{6} \qquad \overset{\div 4}{\frac{8}{12}} = \frac{2}{\boxed{}}$$
$$\div 2 \qquad\qquad\qquad \div 4$$

7. Find the missing numerator or denominator.

(a) $\dfrac{8}{10} = \dfrac{\boxed{}}{5}$

(b) $\dfrac{4}{8} = \dfrac{\boxed{}}{2}$

(c) $\dfrac{6}{9} = \dfrac{\boxed{}}{3}$

(d) $\dfrac{6}{9} = \dfrac{2}{\boxed{}}$

(e) $\dfrac{9}{12} = \dfrac{3}{\boxed{}}$

(f) $\dfrac{10}{12} = \dfrac{5}{\boxed{}}$

8. Find the missing numerator or denominator.

(a) $\dfrac{4}{8} = \dfrac{2}{\boxed{}} = \dfrac{\boxed{}}{2}$

(b) $\dfrac{1}{3} = \dfrac{\boxed{}}{6} = \dfrac{3}{\boxed{}}$

(c) $\dfrac{2}{8} = \dfrac{1}{\boxed{}} = \dfrac{\boxed{}}{12}$

Exercise 5, pages 99—100

9. Complete the following equivalent fractions of $\frac{6}{12}$.

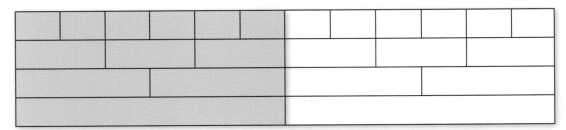

(a) $\frac{6}{12} = \frac{3}{\square}$

(b) $\frac{6}{12} = \frac{2}{\square}$

(c) $\frac{6}{12} = \frac{1}{\square}$

The simplest equivalent fraction of $\frac{6}{12}$ is $\frac{\square}{\square}$.

10. Express each of the following fractions in its simplest form.

(a) $\frac{2}{4}$

(b) $\frac{6}{8}$

(c) $\frac{5}{10}$

(d) $\frac{3}{9}$

(e) $\frac{4}{10}$

(f) $\frac{4}{6}$

(g) $\frac{10}{12}$

(h) $\frac{6}{10}$

Exercise 6, pages 101–102

11. Which is greater, $\frac{3}{4}$ or $\frac{5}{8}$?

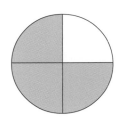

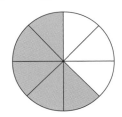

$\frac{3}{4} = \frac{\square}{8}$

12. Which is greater, $\frac{2}{5}$ or $\frac{7}{10}$?

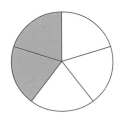

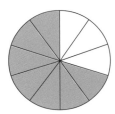

$\frac{2}{5} = \frac{\square}{10}$

96

13. Use > or <.

$\frac{5}{6}$ m ⬤ $\frac{6}{7}$ m

Which is closer to 1 m?

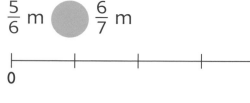

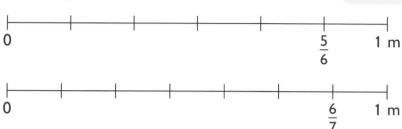

14. Each pair of fractions is for the same whole.
Put > or < between each pair.

(a) $\frac{2}{3}$ ⬤ $\frac{5}{6}$ (b) $\frac{3}{8}$ ⬤ $\frac{1}{2}$ (c) $\frac{3}{5}$ ⬤ $\frac{7}{10}$

(d) $\frac{4}{5}$ ⬤ $\frac{7}{10}$ (e) $\frac{11}{12}$ ⬤ $\frac{5}{6}$ (f) $\frac{2}{3}$ ⬤ $\frac{5}{9}$

15. Each set of fractions is for the same whole.
Arrange the fractions in order, beginning with the smallest.

(a) $\frac{5}{8}$, $\frac{1}{2}$, $\frac{3}{4}$ (b) $\frac{3}{10}$, $\frac{3}{5}$, $\frac{2}{5}$

16. Jackie ate $\frac{3}{8}$ of a pizza.

Marco ate $\frac{1}{4}$ of the same pizza.
Who ate less pizza?

⬜ ate less pizza.

17. A pine tree sapling is $\frac{2}{5}$ m tall.
A maple tree sapling next to it is $\frac{5}{10}$ m tall.
Which one is taller?

The ⬜ sapling is taller.

Exercise 7, page 103

3 Fractions and Measurement

There are two and a half watermelons.

2 and $\frac{1}{2}$ is $2\frac{1}{2}$.

There are $2\frac{1}{2}$ watermelons.

If each whole watermelon was cut in half, would each half be exactly the same?

Each strip of paper measures $\frac{1}{2}$ m.
How long are 3 such strips put end to end?

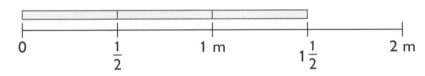

0          $\frac{1}{2}$ 1 m $1\frac{1}{2}$ 2 m

They are $1\frac{1}{2}$ m long.

Is each half of a meter exactly the same length?

The total amount of water is $3\frac{3}{4}$ liters.

3 and $\frac{3}{4}$ is $3\frac{3}{4}$.

1. Each weight has a mass of $\frac{1}{2}$ kg.
   What is the mass of the package?

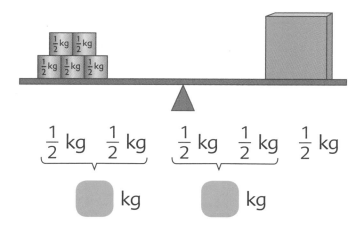

$\frac{1}{2}$ kg $\frac{1}{2}$ kg $\frac{1}{2}$ kg $\frac{1}{2}$ kg $\frac{1}{2}$ kg

[ ] kg   [ ] kg

The mass of the package is [ ] kg.

2. Rod A is 1 m long.
   What are the lengths of the other rods?

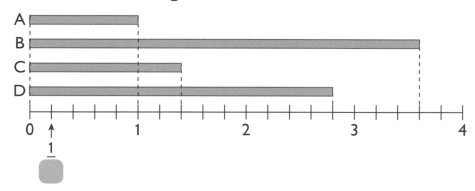

(a) Rod B is [ ] m long.

(b) Rod C is [ ] m long.

(c) Rod D is [ ] m long.

(d) Which of the rods are shorter than 2 m?

(e) Which of the rods are longer than $2\frac{1}{2}$ m?

3. How long is the line?

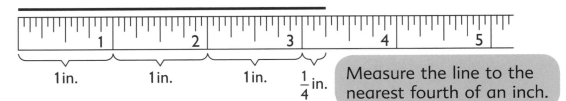

1 in.   1 in.   1 in. $\frac{1}{4}$ in.

Measure the line to the nearest fourth of an inch.

The line is ⬚ in. long.

4. Fill in the missing numerators.

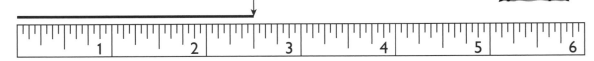

$2\frac{\square}{16}$ in. $= 2\frac{\square}{8}$ in. $= 2\frac{\square}{4}$ in. $= 2\frac{\square}{2}$ in.

The line is $2\frac{\square}{2}$ in. long.

5. How long is the line?

Write measurements in simplest form.

The line is ⬚ in. long.

Exercise 8, pages 104–105

6. (a) How many halves are there in 2?

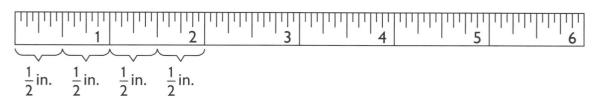

$\frac{1}{2}$ in. $\frac{1}{2}$ in. $\frac{1}{2}$ in. $\frac{1}{2}$ in.

There are ⬜ halves in 2.

$$\frac{1}{2} + \frac{1}{2} + \frac{1}{2} + \frac{1}{2} = \frac{⬜}{2} = 2$$

(b) How many fourths are there in 2?

$$\frac{1}{4} + \frac{1}{4} + \frac{1}{4} + \frac{1}{4} + \frac{1}{4} + \frac{1}{4} + \frac{1}{4} + \frac{1}{4} = \frac{⬜}{4} = 2$$

There are ⬜ fourths in 2.

1 = 4 fourths
2 = 2 x 4 fourths

(c) Fill in the missing numerators.

$$2 = \frac{⬜}{2} = \frac{⬜}{4} = \frac{⬜}{8} = \frac{⬜}{16}$$

7. Write 3 as twelfths.

1 = 12 twelfths
3 = 3 x 12 twelfths

$$3 = \frac{⬜}{12}$$

8. Find the equivalent fractions for the whole numbers.

(a) $2 = \frac{⬜}{5}$ (b) $4 = \frac{⬜}{3}$ (c) $6 = \frac{⬜}{4}$

(d) $5 = \frac{⬜}{8}$ (e) $3 = \frac{⬜}{9}$ (f) $5 = \frac{⬜}{100}$

9. Fill in the missing numerator or denominator.

(a) $4 = \frac{⬜}{1}$ (b) $6 = \frac{6}{⬜}$ (c) $9 = \frac{⬜}{1}$

Exercise 9, page 106

4 Fraction of a Set

1 out of 4 kittens is black.
What fraction of the kittens are black?
$\frac{1}{4}$ of the kittens are black.

1 out of the 4 equal groups of kittens is black.

What fraction of the kittens are black?
$\frac{1}{4}$ of the kittens are black.

What fraction of the kittens are white?

1.

   □/□ of the apples are red.

   There are 3 equal parts in this set of apples.
   1 part is a red apple.
   $\frac{1}{3}$ is 1 out of the 3 equal parts.

2.

   □/□ of the flowers are sunflowers.

   There are 5 flowers.
   2 of the 5 flowers are sunflowers.

   What fraction of the flowers are not sunflowers?

3. There are 8 pieces of fruit in a set. $\frac{3}{8}$ of the pieces of fruit are pears. The rest are bananas.

   □/□ of the pieces of fruit are bananas.

   $\frac{3}{8}$ and □/□ is 1 whole set of fruit.

4. Sam buys 5 toys.
   Two of his toys are cars.
   The rest are planes.
   What fraction of the toys are cars?

5. Sally has 4 ribbons.
   1 of the ribbons is red.
   The rest are blue.
   What fraction of the ribbons are blue?

Exercise 10, pages 107–108

103

6. There are 12 animals. 8 of them are rabbits. The rest are sheep.

(a)

 of 12 animals are sheep.

$\frac{\boxed{}}{12}$ of the animals are sheep.

(b)

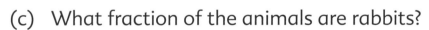 part out of the 3 parts is sheep. $\frac{4}{12} = \frac{1}{3}$

$\frac{\boxed{}}{3}$ of the animals are sheep.

(c) What fraction of the animals are rabbits?

(d) What fraction of the animals are white?

7. What fraction of the children are girls?

$\frac{\boxed{}}{\boxed{}}$ of the children are girls.

104

8. There are 10 oranges on a tree.
   Miguel picked 2 of them.
   What fraction of the oranges did he pick?

2 oranges out of 10 oranges $= \dfrac{\Box}{10} = \dfrac{\Box}{\Box}$

He picked $\dfrac{\Box}{\Box}$ of the oranges.

9. Amy has 12 coins.
   3 of them are pennies.

What fraction of the coins are pennies?

10.

(a) What fraction of the apples are green? $\dfrac{6}{10} = \dfrac{3}{5}$

$\dfrac{3}{5}$ of the apples are green.

6 green apples out of the 10 apples in total

(b) $\dfrac{\Box}{\Box}$ of the apples are red.

$\dfrac{3}{5} + \dfrac{\Box}{\Box} = 1$ whole (all the apples)

11. What fraction of each set is blue?

(a)

(b)

(c)

(d)

(e)

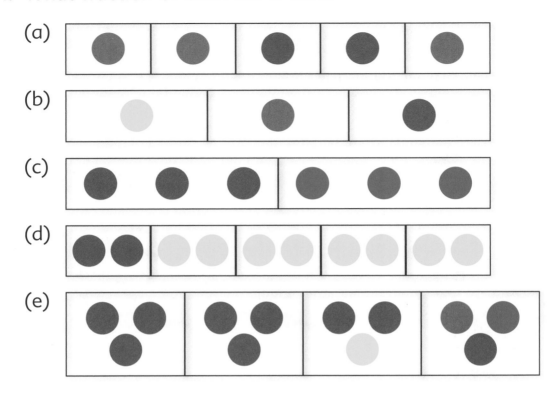

12. What fraction of the apples are green?

(a)

(b)

(c)

(d)

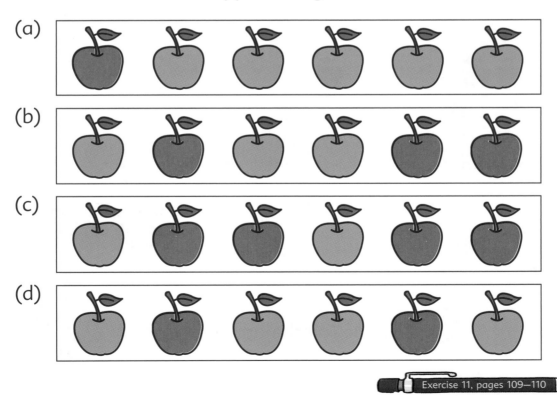

Exercise 11, pages 109—110

1. Which fraction of the shape is not shaded?

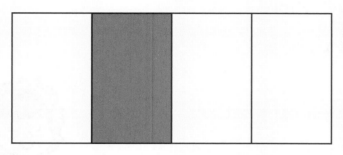

   (A) $\frac{1}{4}$ (B) $\frac{2}{4}$ (C) $\frac{3}{4}$ (D) 3

2. Which of the following fractions is the same as 2 wholes?

   (A) $\frac{2}{2}$ (B) $\frac{4}{8}$ (C) $\frac{6}{2}$ (D) $\frac{8}{4}$

3. What is the fraction represented by A on the number line?

   (A) $\frac{1}{6}$ (B) $\frac{1}{7}$ (C) $\frac{5}{6}$ (D) $\frac{6}{7}$

4. Select True or False.

   (a) $\frac{4}{1} = 4$ True / False

   (b) $\frac{5}{6} < \frac{6}{6}$ True / False

5. Select True or False.

   (a) $\frac{1}{8} > \frac{1}{2}$ True / False

   (b) $\frac{1}{3} + \frac{1}{3} + \frac{1}{3} = 1$ True / False

6. Find the missing fractions.

   (a) $\frac{1}{4}$ and ▢ make 1 whole.

   (b) $\frac{3}{10}$ and ▢ make 1 whole.

   (c) $\frac{7}{12}$ and ▢ make 1 whole.

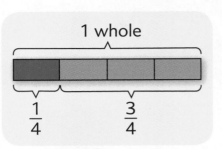

1 whole

$\frac{1}{4}$ $\frac{3}{4}$

7. Name the numerator of each fraction.

   (a) $\frac{2}{3}$ (b) $\frac{6}{10}$ (c) $\frac{9}{12}$

8. Name the denominator of each fraction.

   (a) $\frac{5}{8}$ (b) $\frac{4}{9}$ (c) $\frac{7}{10}$

9. Which fraction is greater?

   (a) $\frac{2}{5}$ or $\frac{4}{5}$ (b) $\frac{1}{4}$ or $\frac{1}{6}$ (c) $\frac{3}{8}$ or $\frac{3}{5}$

10. Which fraction is smaller?

   (a) $\frac{7}{10}$ or $\frac{3}{10}$ (b) $\frac{1}{8}$ or $\frac{1}{10}$ (c) $\frac{2}{9}$ or $\frac{2}{3}$

11. Which is the greatest fraction?

   (a) $\frac{4}{7}$, $\frac{1}{7}$, $\frac{5}{7}$ (b) $\frac{1}{4}$, $\frac{1}{2}$, $\frac{1}{5}$

12. Which is the smallest fraction?

   (a) $\frac{5}{6}$, $\frac{1}{6}$, $\frac{4}{6}$ (b) $\frac{3}{9}$, $\frac{3}{5}$, $\frac{3}{10}$

13. Find the missing numerator in each of the following.

(a) $\dfrac{1}{4} = \dfrac{\square}{8}$ (b) $\dfrac{3}{5} = \dfrac{\square}{15}$ (c) $\dfrac{1}{3} = \dfrac{\square}{6} = \dfrac{\square}{9}$

(d) $\dfrac{4}{10} = \dfrac{\square}{5}$ (e) $\dfrac{6}{9} = \dfrac{\square}{3}$ (f) $\dfrac{1}{2} = \dfrac{\square}{4} = \dfrac{\square}{6}$

14. Find the missing denominator in each of the following.

(a) $\dfrac{2}{5} = \dfrac{4}{\square}$ (b) $\dfrac{3}{4} = \dfrac{9}{\square}$ (c) $\dfrac{2}{3} = \dfrac{4}{\square} = \dfrac{6}{\square}$

(d) $\dfrac{6}{12} = \dfrac{1}{\square}$ (e) $\dfrac{6}{8} = \dfrac{3}{\square}$ (f) $\dfrac{1}{2} = \dfrac{3}{\square} = \dfrac{5}{\square}$

15. Find the missing numerator or denominator.

(a) $\dfrac{1}{4} = \dfrac{\square}{12}$ (b) $\dfrac{2}{3} = \dfrac{6}{\square}$ (c) $\dfrac{8}{10} = \dfrac{4}{\square}$

16. Circle the greater fraction.

(a) $\dfrac{3}{10}, \dfrac{7}{10}$ (b) $\dfrac{5}{6}, \dfrac{9}{12}$ (c) $\dfrac{9}{10}, \dfrac{4}{5}$

(d) $\dfrac{1}{2}, \dfrac{5}{6}$ (e) $\dfrac{7}{12}, \dfrac{2}{3}$ (f) $\dfrac{3}{4}, \dfrac{5}{8}$

17. Which sign goes in the ⬤, > or <?

(a) $\dfrac{1}{3}$ ⬤ $\dfrac{1}{4}$ (b) $\dfrac{2}{7}$ ⬤ $\dfrac{4}{7}$ (c) $\dfrac{10}{10}$ ⬤ $\dfrac{11}{12}$

(d) $\dfrac{3}{4}$ ⬤ $\dfrac{5}{8}$ (e) $\dfrac{2}{5}$ ⬤ $\dfrac{3}{10}$ (f) $\dfrac{3}{6}$ ⬤ $\dfrac{2}{3}$

18. Arrange the fractions in order, beginning with the smallest fraction.

(a) $\dfrac{3}{7}, \dfrac{1}{7}, \dfrac{5}{7}$ (b) $\dfrac{1}{5}, \dfrac{1}{2}, \dfrac{1}{10}$

(c) $\dfrac{2}{3}, \dfrac{1}{2}, \dfrac{5}{6}$ (d) $\dfrac{2}{3}, \dfrac{1}{4}, \dfrac{5}{12}$

19. Melissa ate $\frac{2}{6}$ of a pie.

Sara ate $\frac{1}{2}$ of the pie.

Who ate a bigger portion of the pie?

20. Give each answer in its simplest form.

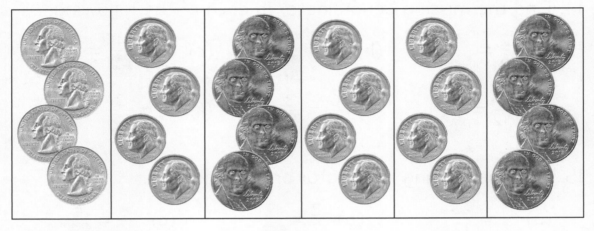

(a) What fraction of the coins are quarters?
(b) What fraction of the coins are dimes?
(c) What fraction of the coins are nickels?

21. What fraction of each set of balls is striped?
Give each answer in its simplest form.

(a)

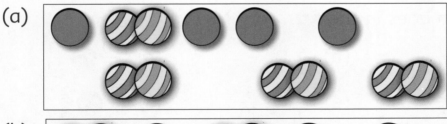

(b)

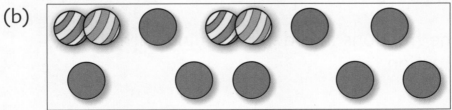

22. Juan spent $\frac{4}{9}$ of his allowance and saved the rest.

What fraction of his allowance did he save?

23. Mary has a tape that is 1 foot long.

She cuts it into smaller pieces each 2 inches long.

Each smaller piece is what fraction of the whole tape?

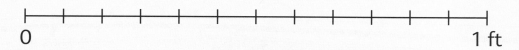

0   1 ft

24. How many sixths are there in 6?

25. How many fourths of an inch are there in 5 inches?

26. Which is greater, $\frac{1}{3}$ or $\frac{4}{12}$?

Ian says that $\frac{4}{12}$ is greater because both the numerators and denominators are larger.

Is Ian correct?

Explain your answer using drawings.

Review 9, pages 111–114

10 TIME

1 Hours and Minutes

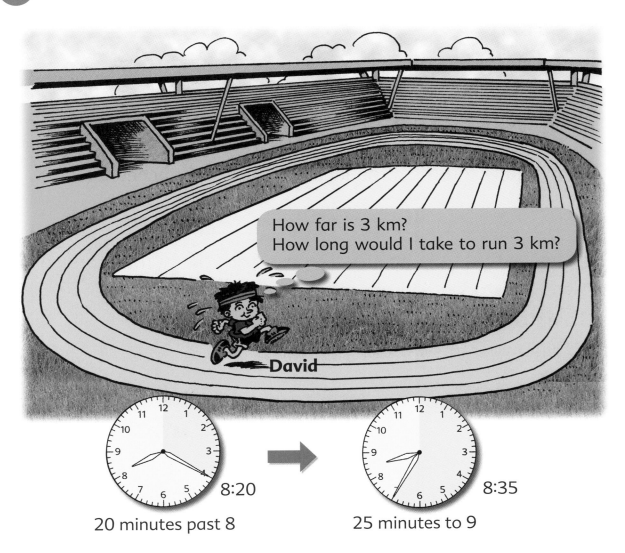

How far is 3 km?
How long would I take to run 3 km?

David

8:20
20 minutes past 8

8:35
25 minutes to 9

David started running at 8:20 A.M.
He ran 3 km.
He finished at 8:35 A.M.
He took 15 minutes to run 3 km.

We read 8:35 as **eight thirty-five**. 8:35 is 25 minutes **before** 9 o'clock. We say the time is twenty-five minutes **to** nine.

We read 8:20 as **eight twenty**. 8:20 is 20 minutes **after** 8 o'clock. We say the time is twenty minutes **past** eight.

1. Find out how many times you can write your name in 1 minute.

2. What time is it?

(a)

(b)

(c)

(d)

(e)

(f)

Exercise 1, pages 115—116

A.M. means after 12:00 midnight and before 12:00 noon.
P.M. means after 12:00 noon and before 12:00 midnight.

3. What time is 26 minutes after 9:30 A.M.?

26 minutes later

4. How many minutes are there in **1 hour**?

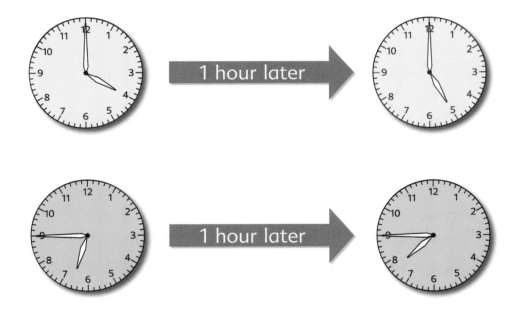

1 hour later

1 hour later

The **hour (h)** and **minute (min)** are units of time.

1 hour = 60 minutes

5. (a) How many **minutes** are there from 1:15 P.M. to 1:42 P.M.?

(b) How many **hours** are there from 3:18 P.M. to 8:18 P.M.?

(c) How long is it from 9:15 A.M. to 11:30 A.M.?

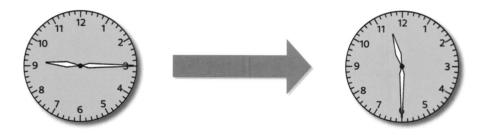

(d) How long is it from 10:45 A.M. to 1:15 P.M.?

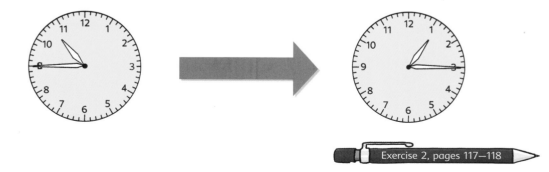

Exercise 2, pages 117—118

6. The table shows the time taken by three children to paint a picture.

   (a) Who took the longest time?
   (b) Who took the shortest time?

Name	Time taken
Amy	1 h 15 min
Jane	2 h 5 min
Sue	1 h 20 min

7. Marcus took 1 h 35 min to complete a jigsaw puzzle. Write the time taken in minutes.

   1 h 35 min = ⬜ min

   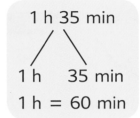

   1 h 35 min
   1 h   35 min
   1 h = 60 min

8. Write in minutes.
   (a) 2 h
   (b) 2 h 10 min
   (c) 2 h 45 min
   (d) 3 h
   (e) 3 h 5 min
   (f) 3 h 15 min

9. Ms. Lean sewed 4 sets of curtains.
   She took 50 min to sew each set of curtains.
   Find the total time taken in hours and minutes.

   50 min × 4 = 200 min

   200 min = ⬜ h ⬜ min

   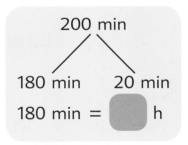

   200 min
   180 min   20 min
   180 min = ⬜ h

10. Write in hours and minutes.
    (a) 70 min
    (b) 85 min
    (c) 100 min
    (d) 125 min
    (e) 160 min
    (f) 210 min

Exercise 3, pages 119–120

116

11. A plane left San Francisco at 8:00 A.M.
It arrived in Portland at 9:05 A.M.
How long did the journey take?

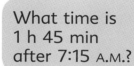

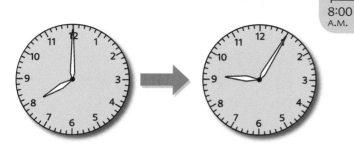

The journey took ◻ h ◻ min.

12. Kristi went to the market at 7:15 A.M.
She came home 1 h 45 min later.
When did she come home?

What time is
1 h 45 min
after 7:15 A.M.?

She came home at ◻ A.M.

13. Sally took 1 h 10 min to do her homework.
She finished doing her homework at 9:40 P.M.
When did she start?

What time is
1 h 10 min
before 9:40 P.M.?

10 min   1 h
├──────────┼──────────┤
?   8:40 A.M.   9:40 A.M.

She started at ◻ P.M.

Exercise 4, pages 121–122

117

14. Fill in the blanks.

| 10:45 | 11:00 | 12:00 | | 2:00 | 3:00 | 3:30 |
| A.M. | A.M | noon | | P.M. | P.M. | P.M. |

(a) 2:00 P.M. is ⬜ h after 12:00 noon.

(b) 3:30 P.M. is ⬜ h ⬜ min after 12:00 noon.

(c) 10:45 A.M. is ⬜ h ⬜ min before 12:00 noon.

15. A supermarket is open from 10:15 A.M. to 9:30 P.M. every day.
How long is the supermarket open a day?

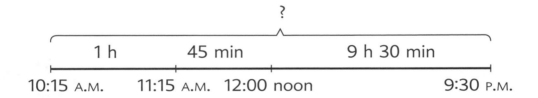

| 1 h | 45 min | 9 h 30 min |

| 10:15 A.M. | 11:15 A.M. | 12:00 noon | 9:30 P.M. |

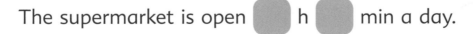

1 h 45 min $\xrightarrow{+9\,h}$ 10 h 45 min $\xrightarrow{+30\,min}$ 11 h 15 min

1 h 45 min + 9 h 30 min = ⬜ h ⬜ min

The supermarket is open ⬜ h ⬜ min a day.

118

16. Fill in the blanks.

| 9:10 P.M. | 10:00 P.M | 12:00 midnight | 4:00 A.M. | 6:00 A.M. | 6:40 A.M. |

(a) 4:00 A.M. is ⬜ h after 12:00 midnight.

(b) 6:40 A.M. is ⬜ h ⬜ min after 12:00 midnight.

(c) 9:10 P.M. is ⬜ h ⬜ min before 12:00 midnight.

17. A night tour began at 10:30 P.M. and lasted 3 h 20 min. When did the night tour end?

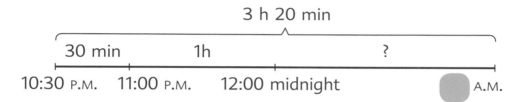

3 h 20 min

30 min   1h   ?

10:30 P.M.   11:00 P.M.   12:00 midnight   ⬜ A.M.

3 h 20 min —1 h→ 2 h 20 min —30 min→ 1 h 50 min

3 h 20 min − 1 h 30 min = ⬜ h ⬜ min

The night tour ended at ⬜ A.M.

18. Add or subtract.
    (a) 2 h 40 min + 3 h
    (b) 2 h 20 min + 45 min
    (c) 3 h 15 min − 2 h
    (d) 3 h 5 min − 30 min
    (e) 1 h 25 min + 2 h 15 min
    (f) 2 h 40 min + 2 h 25 min
    (g) 3 h 50 min − 1 h 35 min
    (h) 3 h 20 min + 1 h 40 min

19. David took 2 h 35 min to repair a van and 1 h 55 min to repair a car.

   (a) How long did he take to repair both vehicles?

   He took ▢ to repair both vehicles.

   (b) How much longer did he take to repair the van than the car?

   He took ▢ longer to repair the van than the car.

20. Cameron took 2 h 30 min to paint his room.
   He began at 9:20 A.M.
   What time did he finish painting his room?

   He finished painting his room at ▢.

21. A group of children left for a field trip at 8:30 A.M.
   They returned 4 h 10 min later.
   What time did they return?

   They returned at ▢.

22. A supermarket opens for business at 9:30 A.M.
   Its workers have to report for work 40 minutes earlier.
   What time must the workers report for work?

   The workers must report for work at ▢.

Exercise 3, pages 123–124

2 Other Units of Time

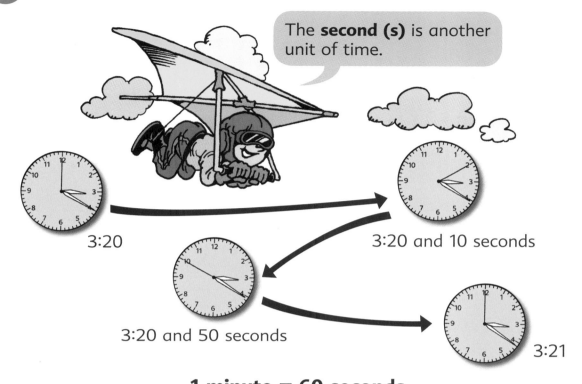

The **second (s)** is another unit of time.

3:20

3:20 and 10 seconds

3:20 and 50 seconds

3:21

1 minute = 60 seconds

1. (a) Find out how many times you can skip in 10 seconds.

(b) How long do you take to write the word CHILDREN?
(c) How long do you take to run 100 m?

Exercise 6, pages 125–126

The hour (h), minute (min), and second (s) are units of time.

1 h = 60 min
1 min = 60 s

2. Write 3 min 40 s in seconds.

3 min 40 s = s

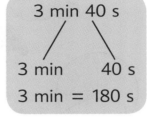

3. Write in seconds.
   (a) 2 min (b) 2 min 20 s (c) 2 min 45 s
   (d) 4 min (e) 4 min 5 s   (f) 4 min 37 s

4. Write 150 s in minutes and seconds.

150 s = [ ] min [ ] s

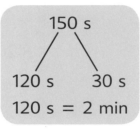

5. Write in minutes and seconds.
   (a) 80 s   (b) 95 s   (c) 105 s
   (d) 128 s   (e) 150 s   (f) 204 s

6. Sandra ran the first half of the relay in
   6 min 12 s. Connie ran the second half of the
   relay in 3 min 25 s. How much time did they
   take to complete the relay?

6 min 12 s + 3 min 25 s =

6 min 12 s $\xrightarrow{+\,3\ min}$ 9 min 12 s $\xrightarrow{+\,25\ s}$ 9 min 37 s

They took [ ] to complete the relay.

7. Kevin took 8 min 35 s to solve a puzzle.
   Titus took 6 min 50 s to solve the same puzzle.
   How much longer did Kevin take to solve the puzzle?

   8 min 35 s − 6 min 50 s = [ ]

   8 min 35 s $\xrightarrow{-6\ min}$ 2 min 35 s $\xrightarrow{-50\ s}$ 1 min 45 s

   Kevin took [ ] longer to solve the puzzle.

8. Add or subtract.
   (a) 3 min 20 s + 4 min   (b) 3 min 45 s + 20 s
   (c) 5 min 25 s − 3 min   (d) 4 min 5 s − 40 s
   (e) 2 min 15 s + 1 min 35 s   (f) 2 min 55 s + 2 min 20 s
   (g) 3 min 40 s − 1 min 25 s   (h) 3 min 20 s − 1 min 50 s

9. Fill in the missing numbers.

   Exercise 1, pages 127–131

   (a) 1 year = [ ] months

   (b) 2 years = [ ] months

   The **year**, **month**, **week**, and **day** are units of time too.

   (c) 2 years 4 months = [ ] months

   (d) 40 months = [ ] years [ ] months

10. Fill in the missing numbers.

   (a) 1 week = [ ] days

   (b) 3 weeks = [ ] days

   (c) 3 weeks 4 days = [ ] days

   (d) 30 days = [ ] weeks [ ] days

   Exercise 1, pages 132–135

1.

   What time does the clock show?
   (A) 15 minutes to 4
   (B) 15 minutes to 5
   (C) 45 minutes to 5
   (D) 45 minutes past 5

2. Express 3 min 20 s in seconds.
   (A) 200 s
   (B) 320 s
   (C) 2,000 s
   (D) 3,200 s

3. Nadia started practicing her piano at 3:45 P.M.
   She stopped practicing at 5:30 P.M.
   How long did she practice her piano?
   (A) 1 h 45 min
   (B) 2 h 15 min
   (C) 8 h 75 min
   (D) 9 h 15 min

4. Select True or False.
   (A) 20 minutes to 6 is 5:40.   True / False
   (B) 15 minutes to 3 is 3.15.   True / False

5. Select True or False.
   (A) 3 min > 300 s   True / False
   (B) 250 min < 4 h 10 min   True / False

6. Find the missing numbers.

   (a) 2 h 12 min = ⬜ min

   (b) 108 min = ⬜ h ⬜ min

   (c) 2 min 3 s = ⬜ s

   (d) 94 s = ⬜ min ⬜ s

   (e) 1 year 9 months = ⬜ months

   (f) 30 months = ⬜ years ⬜ months

   (g) 2 weeks 5 days = ⬜ days

   (h) 40 days = ⬜ weeks ⬜ days

7. Add or subtract.
   (a) 1 h 45 min + 2 h   (b) 3 h 40 min − 2 h
   (c) 2 h 15 min + 45 min   (d) 3 h − 1 h 45 min
   (e) 1 h 30 min + 1 h 50 min   (f) 2 h 10 min − 1 h 30 min

8. This clock is 5 min slow.
   What is the correct time?

9. A clock shows 3:56.
   The correct time is 6:05.
   How long is the clock slow by?

10. What time is it?
    (a) 8 h 55 min after 12:00 noon
    (b) 1 h 30 min after 12:00 midnight

11. How long is it?
    (a) From 4:40 A.M. to 11:55 A.M.
    (b) From 5:45 P.M. to 7:00 P.M.
    (c) From 10:05 P.M. to 12:00 midnight.
    (d) From 2:40 P.M. to 3:25 P.M.

12. Mr. Thompson drives for 10 minutes, takes 15 minutes
    to park his car and get on the train, rides the train for
    35 minutes, and then walks 5 minutes to get to work.
    How long does it take him to get to work?
    Give your answer in hours and minutes.

13. The flying time from Chicago to Minneapolis is 1 h 35 min
    and from Miami to Chicago is 3 h 15 min.
    How much longer does it take to fly to Miami than to
    Minneapolis?

14. Coby completed a jigsaw puzzle in 1 h 6 min.
    Lily completed the same jigsaw puzzle 10 minutes faster.
    How long did Lily take to complete the jigsaw puzzle?

15. An art lesson started at 5:40 P.M.
    It lasted 45 minutes.
    When did the lesson end?

16. Molly went shopping at 10:20 A.M.
    She returned home 4 hours later.
    When did she return home?

17. Mr. Cole took 8 h 45 min to drive from Los Angeles to San Francisco.
    He arrived there at 2:15 P.M.
    What time did he leave Los Angeles?

18. A bookshop is open from 9:30 A.M. to 5:00 P.M.
    How long is the bookshop open?

19. Larry and his family went to the park for a picnic.
    They left home at 8:30 A.M. and arrived at the park at 9:15 A.M.
    How long did the journey take?

20. Mr. Chen stayed in Japan for 19 months.
    Mr. Lee stayed there for 2 years 4 months.
    Who stayed longer?
    How many months longer?

21. David and Peter added 6 min 50 s to 7 min 55 s.
    Compare their solutions.

David's solution	7 min 55 s $\xrightarrow{+6 \text{ min}}$ 13 min 55 s $\xrightarrow{+50 \text{ s}}$ 14 min 45 s
Peter's solution	7 min 55 s $\xrightarrow{+6 \text{ min}}$ 13 min 55 s $\xrightarrow{+50 \text{ s}}$ 13 min 105 s $\rightarrow$ 14 min 5 s

Whose solution is wrong? Explain your answer.

Review 10, pages 136–137

11 DATA ANALYSIS

1 Presenting Data

Joanne has counted the number of different types of evergreen trees in a park and put the information into a table.

Tree	Number
Douglas Fir	18
Ponderosa Pine	20
Lodgepole Pine	42
Rocky Mountain Juniper	10
Western White Pine	2
Western Hemlock	16

She makes a scaled picture graph to show the number of trees in a nature park.

She wants to have no more than about 10 symbols in each row.

Douglas Fir	🌲🌲🌲🌲🌲
Ponderosa Pine	🌲🌲🌲🌲🌲
Lodgepole Pine	🌲🌲🌲🌲🌲🌲🌲🌲🌲🌲🌲
Rocky Mountain Juniper	🌲🌲🌲
Western White Pine	🌲
Western Hemlock	🌲🌲🌲🌲

Key: 🌲 = 4 trees

If 🌲 represents 4 trees, what does 🌲 represent?

Why did Joanne choose one symbol for 4 trees?

Could she have used a different scale?

Which is the most common type of tree in the park?

Which is the rarest type of tree?

128

1. This table shows the number of cars sold by Patrick in six months.

Month	Number of cars
January	18
February	8
March	15
April	10
May	16
June	5

(a) Decide on a suitable scale for this data and draw a picture graph.

This data can also be presented in a bar graph.

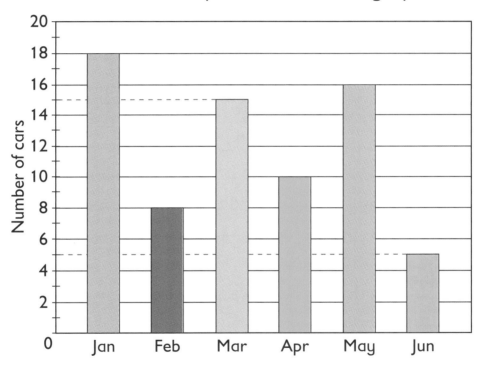

Use the graph to answer the following questions.

(b) In which months did Patrick sell fewer than 10 cars?

(c) How many more cars were sold in May than in April?

(d) In which month were half as many cars sold as in May?

(e) Compare the bar graph to your picture graph.
What are some advantages of presenting data in a bar graph instead of a picture graph?

2. This bar graph shows the number of people who visited a book fair from Monday to Friday.

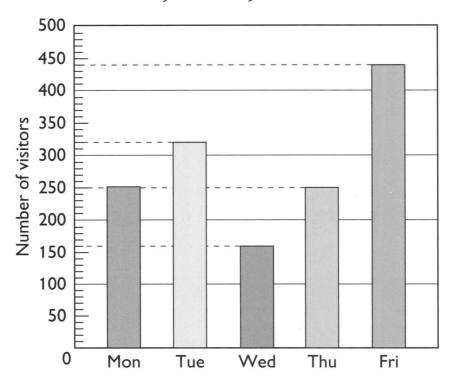

Use the graph to answer the following questions.

(a) How many people visited the book fair on Tuesday?

(b) How many more people visited the book fair on Friday than on Thursday?

(c) On which day were there twice as many visitors as on Wednesday?

(d) If there were 200 adults on Tuesday, how many children were there?

(e) The book fair was open the same hours each day. Which day would be a good day to have the fair open for more hours?

(f) Which day might be a good day to have the book fair open for fewer hours?

(g) What kind of information could be gathered to better answer the last two questions?

3. This bar graph shows the masses of eight children.

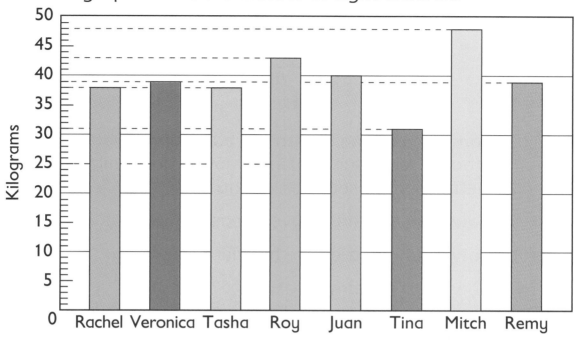

(a) Copy the table below and use the information from the bar graph to complete the table.

Name	Mass
Rachel	
Veronica	
Tasha	
Roy	
Juan	
Tina	
Mitch	
Remy	

(b) Who has the greatest mass?

(c) What is the difference in mass between Mitch and Tina?

Exercise 1, pages 138—144

This same information can be shown in a line plot.

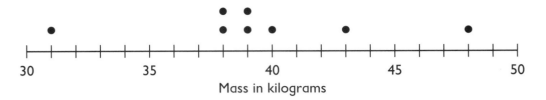

Mass in kilograms

(d) Compare the line plot to the bar graph.
What different kinds of information are available in the two methods of presenting the data?

(e) How many children have a mass of 39 kg?

(f) How many children are heavier than 40 kg?

(g) How many children are lighter than 35 kg?

4. The following line plot shows the height of some saplings in the center and the border of a stand of trees, measured to the nearest half of a foot.

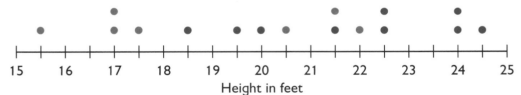

Height in feet

Key: ● = at the border
● = in the center

Use the line plot to answer the following questions.

(a) What is the height of the tallest sapling from the border area?

(b) What is the height of the tallest sapling from the center area?

(c) How many total saplings are shorter than $19\frac{1}{2}$ feet? How many of these are from the center area?

(d) What possible conclusion could you make from this data?

(e) How could you be certain that your conclusion is correct?

5. The following table shows the length of some earthworms measured to the nearest fourth of an inch.

$6\frac{3}{4}$	$7\frac{1}{4}$	13	$11\frac{3}{4}$	$3\frac{1}{2}$
8	$7\frac{1}{4}$	$7\frac{1}{4}$	8	5
$4\frac{3}{4}$	3	$6\frac{1}{2}$	9	$7\frac{3}{4}$
$7\frac{1}{2}$	$7\frac{1}{4}$	5	$8\frac{1}{4}$	$8\frac{3}{4}$

(a) Draw a line plot to show the data.

(b) How many of the earthworms are between $6\frac{1}{2}$ and 9 inches long?

(c) How many are shorter than $6\frac{1}{2}$ inches long?

(d) How many are longer than 9 inches long?

(e) What is the most common length?

6. Measure the height of your classmates to the nearest quarter of a foot and record the data in a table like the one shown below.

Name	Height

(a) Draw a line plot to show the data.

(b) How many of your classmates have heights that are between $4\frac{1}{12}$ and $4\frac{1}{3}$ feet?

(c) How many are shorter than $4\frac{1}{12}$ feet?

(d) How many are taller than $4\frac{1}{3}$ feet?

(e) What is the most common height?

Exercise 2, pages 145–146

This bar graph shows the type of sports students in a school prefer to do on weekends. Each student was asked to choose only one sport.

Use this bar graph to answer questions 1 to 5.

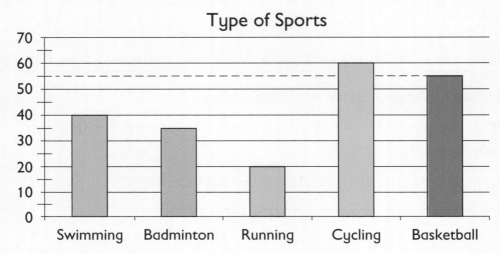

Type of Sports

1. What is the total number of students who prefer to swim or cycle on weekends?
   (A) 75   (B) 60   (C) 95   (D) 100

2. How many more students prefer basketball to running?
   (A) 30   (B) 35   (C) 70   (D) 75

3. How many students are there altogether?
   (A) 185   (B) 200   (C) 210   (D) 215

4. Select True or False.
   (a) There are 5 more students who prefer swimming to badminton.   True / False
   (b) There are 40 fewer students who prefer cycling to running.   True / False

5. Select True or False.
   (a) Badminton is the least preferred sport.   True / False
   (b) Cycling is the most preferred sport.   True / False

6. Fill in the blanks.
   (a) If ▲ stands for 10 people,

   ▲▲▲▲▲◢ stand for [ ] people.

   (b) If ■■■◧ stand for 28 books,

   each ■ stands for [ ] books.

7. This table shows the number of people who attended four courses in a community center.
   Choose a scale and draw a picture graph for this data.

Course	Number of people
Cooking	27
Art	24
Computer	39
Dancing	30

8. The following table shows the lengths of some mature boa constrictors to the nearest fourth of a meter.

5	7	$6\frac{1}{2}$	$7\frac{1}{4}$	$6\frac{1}{4}$
$5\frac{3}{4}$	6	11	$6\frac{1}{4}$	$8\frac{1}{2}$
$6\frac{3}{4}$	$6\frac{1}{4}$	7	$4\frac{3}{4}$	6
$5\frac{3}{4}$	$6\frac{3}{4}$	6	$6\frac{1}{2}$	$6\frac{3}{4}$

Create a line plot of the data and answer the following questions.
(a) What is the length of the shortest boa constrictor?
(b) What is the length of the longest boa constrictor?
(c) What is/are the most common length(s)?
(d) How many more boa constrictors are $6\frac{1}{4}$ m long than 5 m long?

9. This graph shows John's savings in five months.

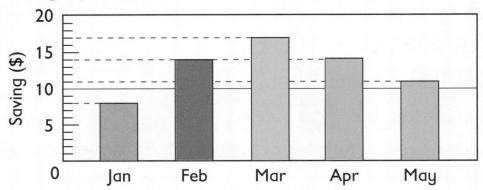

(a) How much did John save in January?

(b) In which month did he save the most?

(c) Find his total savings in the 5 months.

10. The following line plot shows the mass of some third and fourth graders measured to the nearest half of a kilogram.

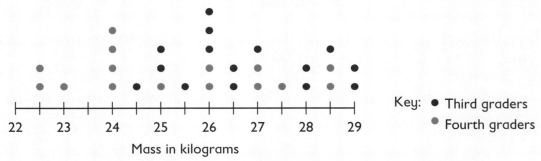

Use the line plot to answer the following questions.

(a) What is the mass of the lightest fourth grader(s)?

(b) What is the mass of the heaviest third grader(s)?

(c) How much heavier is the lightest third grader than the lightest fourth grader?

(d) How much lighter is the heaviest fourth grader than the heaviest third grader?

(e) 4 students had the same mass. How heavy are they?

(f) How many students have a mass of between $22\frac{1}{2}$ kg and $27\frac{1}{2}$ kg?

(g) Sharon's answer for (f) was 23.

Is her answer correct? Explain how she arrived at that answer.

Review 11, pages 147–150

136

12 GEOMETRY

1 Right Angles and Shapes

Use two strips of cardboard and a split pin to form an angle.
Make the angle bigger.
What is the biggest angle you can get?

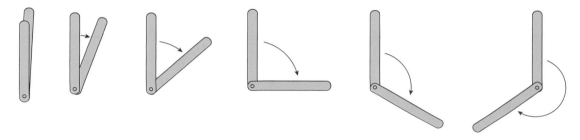

Fold a torn piece of paper twice to make an angle like this:

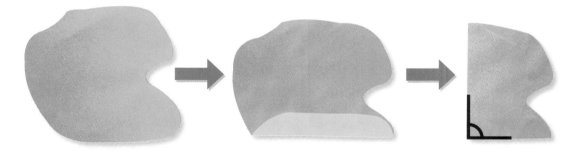

The angle you have made is a special one.
It is a **right angle**.

Use the right angle you have made and make a right angle
with the two pieces of cardboard.

Look for right angles around you.
Check them with the angle you have made.

Get an index card.
Are the corners right angles?

1. Find out which of the following angles are right angles.

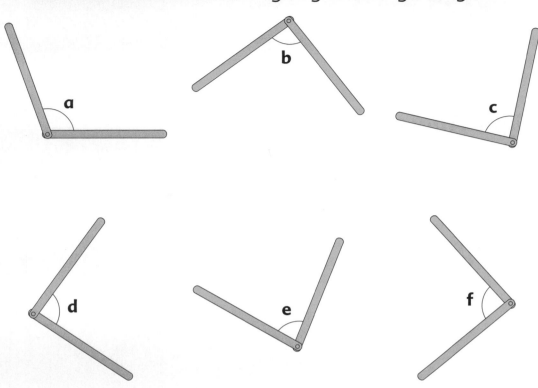

Which angle is greater than a right angle?
Which angle is smaller than a right angle?

2. Draw some angles greater than a right angle.
   Draw some angles smaller than a right angle.

3. Which one of these triangles has a right angle?
   Which one has an angle which is **greater than** a right angle?

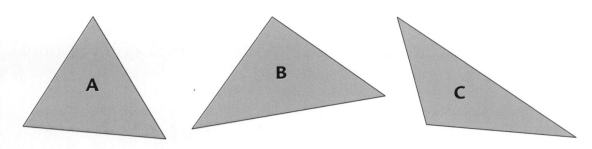

Exercise 1, pages 151–152

4. How many right angles can you find in
   (a) a square?   (b) a rectangle?

A square is a special kind of rectangle.

5. The following figure is called a **rhombus**.
   Measure the sides.

A square is also a special kind of rhombus.

A rhombus has 4 equal sides.
What can you say about the angles in this rhombus?

6. Which of the following figures are rhombuses?

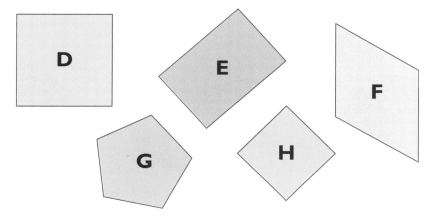

7. Draw a four-sided figure that is **not** a rhombus, rectangle, or square.

139

8. How many angles does each of these figures have?
How many inside angles are right angles?

(a) Quadrilaterals

Rhombuses, squares, and rectangles are quadrilaterals.

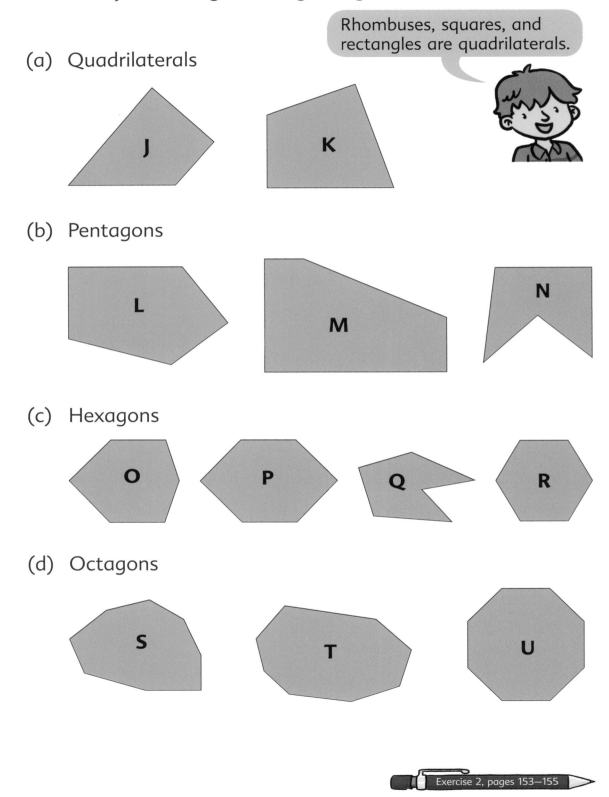

(b) Pentagons

(c) Hexagons

(d) Octagons

Exercise 2, pages 153—155

1. How many angles inside the figure shown below are smaller than a right angle?

    (A) 4   (B) 5   (C) 6   (D) 7

2. Which of these figures have right angles only?

    (A)   (B)

    (C)    (D)

3. Select True or False.
    (a) A pentagon has 5 angles inside.   True / False
    (b) A quadrilateral has right angles only.   True / False

4. Select True or False.
    (a) All rhombuses are squares.   True / False
    (b) All squares are rectangles.   True / False

5. How many angles does each figure have?

(a)

(b)

6. (a) How many right angles does a rectangle have?
   (b) What is the greatest number of right angles a rhombus could have?

7. Look at this figure. Answer the following questions.

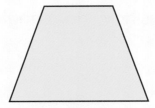

(a) What does a rhombus have that this figure does not?
(b) What does a square have that this figure does not?
(c) What does a rectangle have that this figure does not?
(d) Draw another four-sided figure that is not a rhombus, square, or rectangle.

8. Look at this figure. Answer the following questions.

(a) Is this figure a quadrilateral? Why?
(b) Is this figure a square? Why?
(c) Is this figure a rhombus? Why?
(d) Is this figure a rectangle? Why?

Review 12, pages 156—157

13 AREA AND PERIMETER

1 Area

Make 4 square cards and 4 half-square cards.

Use the cards to make different figures like these:

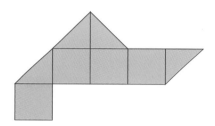

Each ☐ is 1 square unit.

Each ◿ is $\frac{1}{2}$ square unit.

The figures have the same **area**.

The area of each figure is ▢ square units.

2. What is the area of each of the following figures?

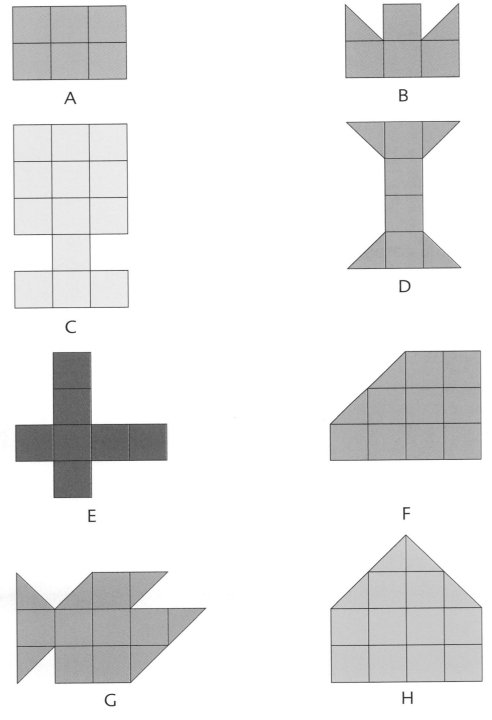

Which figure has the smallest area?
Which figure has the greatest area?

Exercise 1, pages 158—161

144

3. Which two shapes are of the same size?

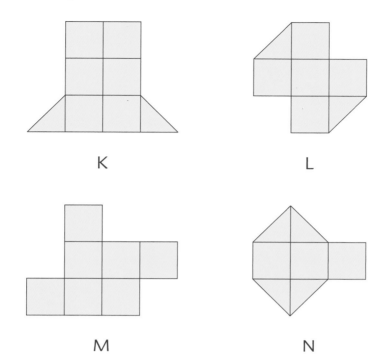

K

L

M

N

4. What is the area of each of the following figures?

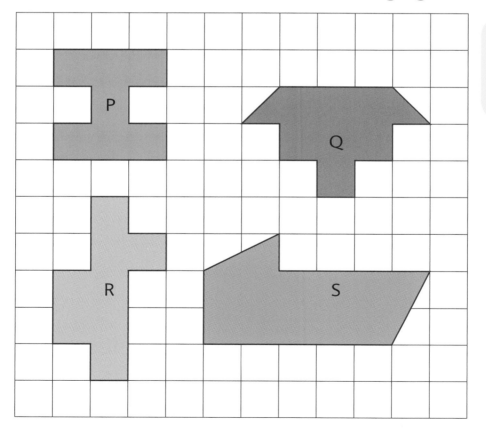

Each ☐ stands for 1 square unit.

5. How many of these 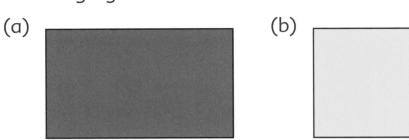 will cover the inside of each of the following figures?

(a)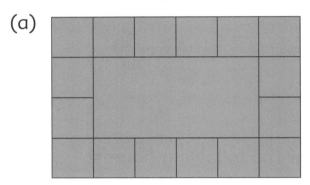

(b)

6. Fill in the missing numbers.

(a)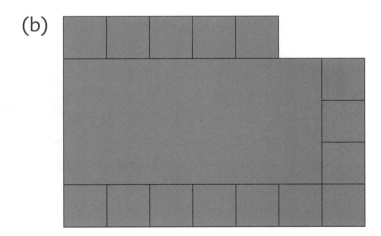

The area of the shape is ⬜ square units.

(b)

The area of the shape is ⬜ square units.

Exercise 2, pages 162–166

7. This is a 1-cm square.

1 cm

1 cm

Each side of the square is 1 cm long.

Its area is 1 **square centimeter**.

Give the area of each of the following squares in square centimeters.

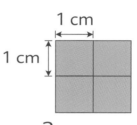

1 cm

1 cm

a 2-cm square

a 3-cm square

a 4-cm square

The square centimeter is a unit of area.

A 2-cm square is made up of 4 pieces of 1-cm squares. Its area is 4 square centimeters.

8. (a) What is the area of a 5-cm square?
   (b) What is the area of a 10-cm square?

9. This figure is made up of 1-cm squares.
   Find its area.

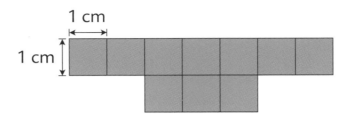

10. What is the area of each of the following figures?

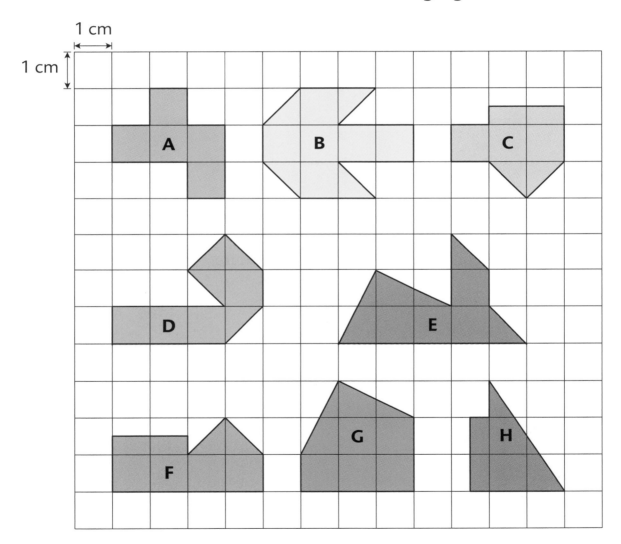

11. Each side of this square is 1 in. long.

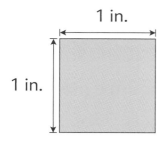

1 in.

1 in.

Its area is 1 **square inch**.

> The square inch is also a unit of area.

Give the area of each of the following figures in square inches.

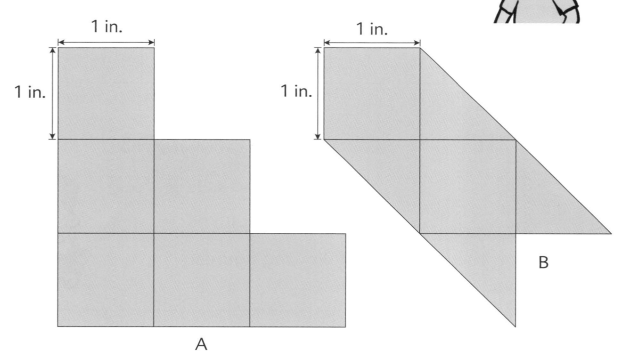

A

B

1 in.

1 in.

1 in.

1 in.

Which figure has the greater area?
Which figure has the smaller area?

12. Each side of this square is 1 m long.

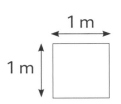

1 m
1 m

When we draw figures, we can make them smaller than the actual size. We label the sides with the actual sizes.

Its area is 1 **square meter**.

What is the area of each of the following figures?

1 m
1 m

A

B

13. Each side of this square is 1 foot long.

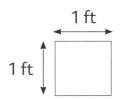

1 ft
1 ft

Square meter and square feet are also units of area.

Its area is 1 **square foot**.

What is the area of the following figures?

1 ft
1 ft

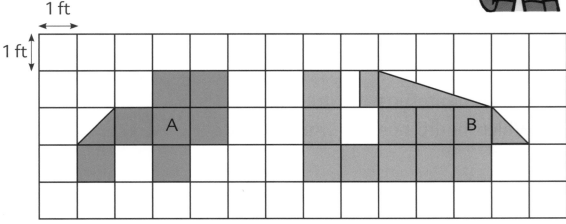

A

B

Exercise 3, pages 167–170

② Perimeter

Sue used 3 pieces of wire of the same length to make the triangle, the square, and the rectangle.

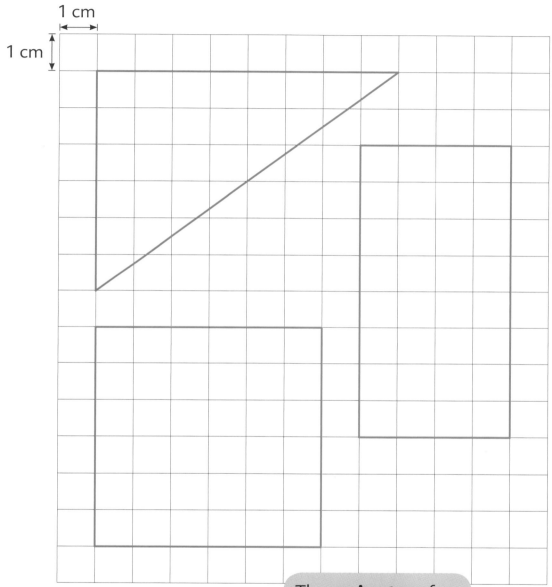

The **perimeter** of a figure is the distance around the figure.

They have the same perimeter.

The perimeter of each figure is cm.

1. Use string to measure the perimeter of each of these figures.

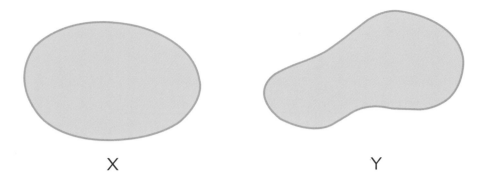

X   Y

Which figure has a longer perimeter?

2. (a) Measure the perimeter of your textbook in centimeters.

   (b) Measure the perimeter of your classroom in meters.

3. These two figures are made up of the same number of 1-cm squares.

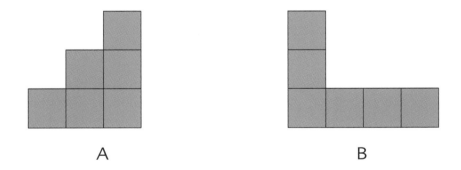

A   B

(a) They have the same area.

   The area of each figure is [ ] square centimeters.

(b) They have different perimeters.

   The perimeter of Figure A is [ ] cm.

   The perimeter of Figure B is [ ] cm.

4. These figures are made up of 1-cm squares.

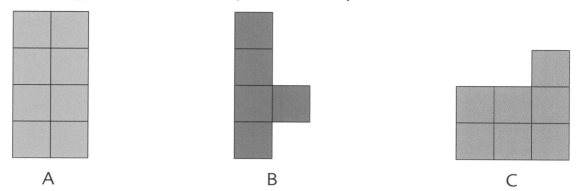

A   B   C

(a) Do they have the same area?

(b) Do they have the same perimeter?

5. These figures are made up of 1-cm squares.

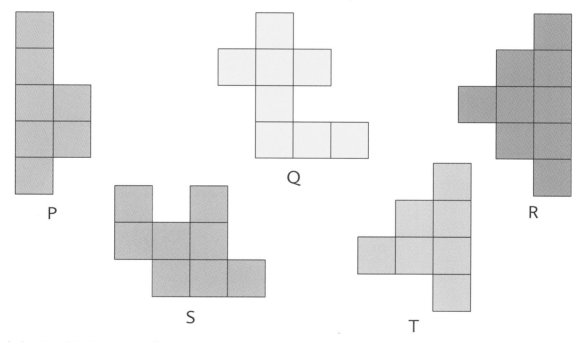

P   Q   R

S   T

(a) Which two figures have the same area but
different perimeters?

(b) Which two figures have the same perimeter but
different areas?

(c) Which two figures have the same area and perimeter?

Exercise 4, pages 171–172

6. (a) Each side of the square is 6 cm long.
   Find its perimeter.

   Perimeter   = 6 + 6 + 6 + 6

               = ⬜ cm

   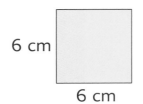

   6 cm

   6 cm

   (b) The length of the rectangle is 12 m.
   Its width is 4 m.
   Find its perimeter.

   Perimeter   = 12 + 4 + 12 + 4

               = ⬜ m

   4 m

   12 m

7. The length of a rectangular field is 85 m and its width is
   10 m. Ian ran around the field once.
   How far did he run?

8. Find the perimeter of each of the following figures:

When we draw figures, we can make them smaller than
the actual size. We label the sides with the actual sizes.

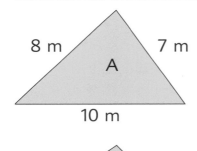

8 m   A   7 m

10 m

9 in.

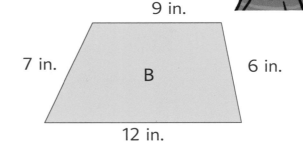

7 in.   B   6 in.

12 in.

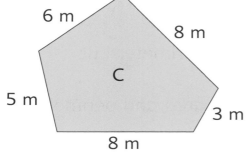

6 m

8 m

C

5 m

3 m

8 m

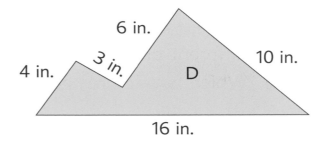

6 in.

3 in.   10 in.

4 in.   D

16 in.

9. The perimeter of the square is 36 in. Find the length of each side.

 Perimeter = 36 in.

Length = 36 ÷ 4

= ⬜ in.

⬜ + ⬜ + ⬜ + ⬜ = 36?

The length of each side of the square is ⬜ in.

10. The perimeter of the rectangle is 40 m. Its length is 13 m. Find its width.

13 m
? Perimeter = 40 m

2 widths = 40 m − 13 m − 13 m
= 14 m
1 width = 14 m ÷ 2

= ⬜ m

13 + ⬜ + 13 + ⬜ = 40

Its width is ⬜ m.

11. The perimeter of a rectangle is 38 in. Its width is 9 in. Find its length.

12. Find the missing side length of each of the following figures:

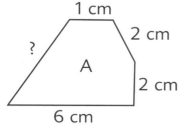
1 cm
2 cm
?
A
2 cm
6 cm
Perimeter = 15 cm

5 m 8 m
B
?
Perimeter = 23 m

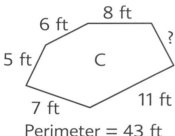
6 ft 8 ft
5 ft
C
?
7 ft 11 ft
Perimeter = 43 ft

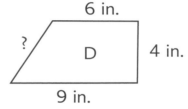
6 in.
?
D 4 in.
9 in.
Perimeter = 24 in.

Exercise 5, pages 173–174

155

3 Area of a Rectangle

Find the area of each of the following rectangles.

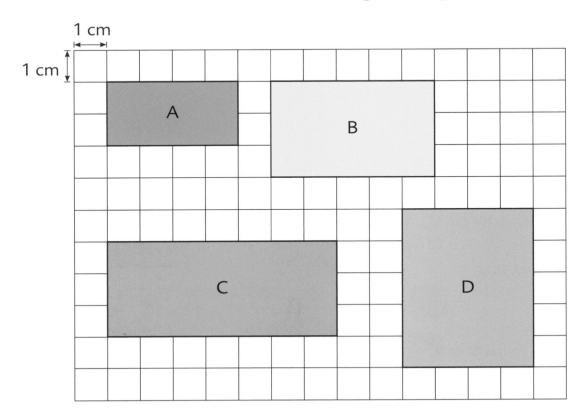

I count the square units covered by each rectangle to find its area.

I multiply the length and width of each rectangle to find its area.

Area of rectangle = Length × Width

1. Find the area of the rectangle.

Area of rectangle
= 5 × 4

= ▢ square units

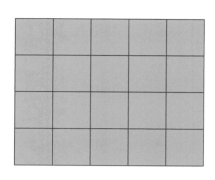

2. Find the area of each of the following rectangles.

(a)
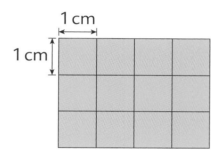

(b)
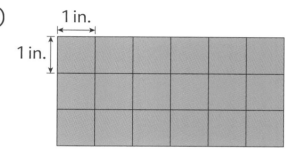

(c)
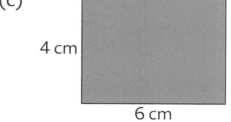

(d)

(e)
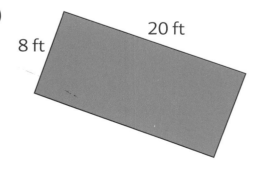

3. Wayne wants to tile his bathroom floor. How many 1-square foot tiles does he need?

Area = length × width

    = 9 ft × 7 ft

    = ⬜ square feet

He needs ⬜ 1-square foot tiles.

4. Mr. Hill wants to lay his rectangular school field with pieces of 1-square meter grass. The length of the school field is 12 m. The width is 8 m. How many such pieces does he need?

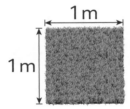

1 m

1 m

5. The length of a square study room is 6 ft.

Find the area of the study room.

6. The length and width of a swimming pool is 50 m and 25 m, respectively.

What is the area of the swimming pool?

7. Candice wants to paste 1-square inch stickers on a card that is 5 in. long and 4 in. wide. How many 1-square inch stickers does she need?

8. This rectangle is made up of 1-cm squares.

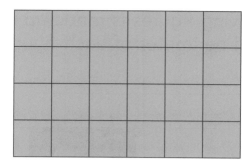

(a) Find the area and perimeter.

(b) Use square cards to find other rectangles with the same area.
   Write down the length, width, and perimeter of each one.
   Compare your rectangles to your friends' rectangles.

9. These two rectangles have the same area.

(a) What is the width of Rectangle B?

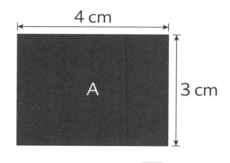

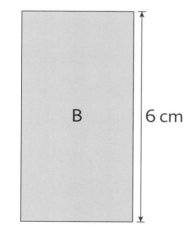

Area of A = ⬜ square centimeters

Area of B = ⬜ square centimeters

⬜ cm × 6 cm = 12 square centimeters

Width of B = ⬜ cm

(b) What is the perimeter of Rectangle B?

Exercise 6, pages 175–177

4 Composite Figures

Each of the following figures is made up of two rectangles. Find the area and perimeter of each figure.

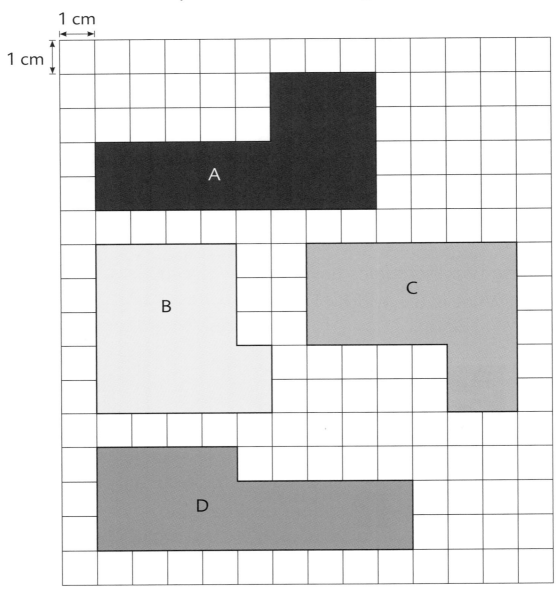

Do the figures have the same area?
Do they have the same perimeter?

1. The figure below is made up of a rectangle and a square. Find the perimeter and the area of the entire figure.

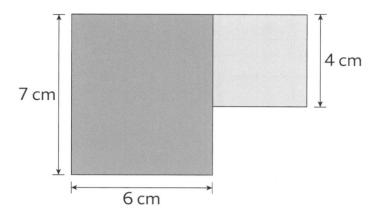

2. A square was cut out of a rectangular piece of carpeting in order to carpet an L-shaped room.

Find the area and perimeter of the piece of carpet.

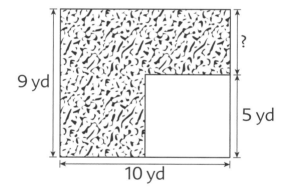

The carpet is made up of a square and a rectangle. I found their areas and added them together.

I found the area of the uncut carpet and then subtracted the area of the square part.

The area of the carpet is square yards.

3. What are the areas of these rectangles?

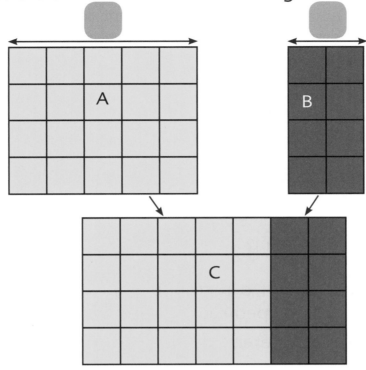

(a) Area of rectangle A = 4 units × ⬜ units

= ⬜ square units

Area of rectangle B = 4 units × ⬜ units

= ⬜ square units

Total area = Area of rectangle A + Area of rectangle B

= ⬜ square units + ⬜ square units

= ⬜ square units

$$5 + 2 = 7$$
$$(4 \times 5) + (4 \times 2) = 4 \times 7$$

(b) Length of rectangle C = ⬜ units + ⬜ units

= ⬜ units

Area of rectangle C = 4 units × ⬜ units

= ⬜ square units

4. Mark has 2 pieces of poster paper. Each has one side that is 9 in. long.

He puts them together to make a longer poster.

What is the area of his poster?

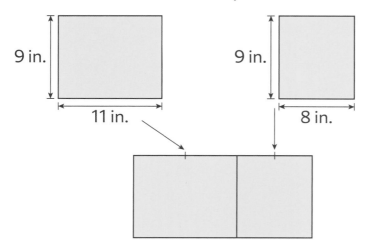

I found the area of each piece first.

(a) 9 in. × 11 in. = ☐ square inches

   9 in. × 8 in. = ☐ square inches

   Total area = ☐ square inches + ☐ square inches

   = ☐ square inches

(b) 11 in. + 8 in. = ☐ in.

   Total area = 9 in. × ☐ in. = ☐ square inches

I found the total length first.

5. Each figure is made up of squares and rectangles.
   Find the area and perimeter of each.

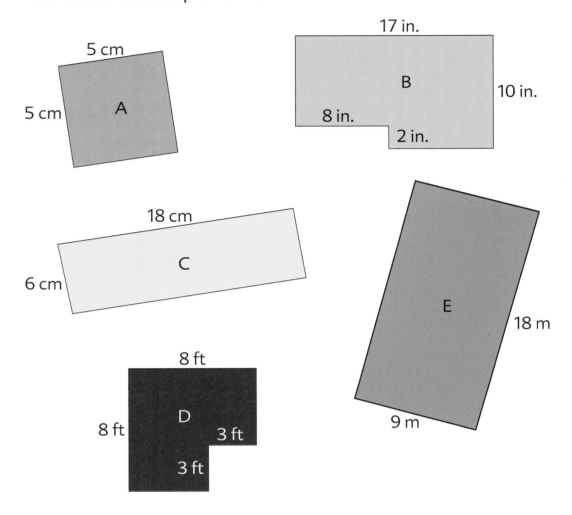

6. Mr. Cheng wants to lay carpet over
   his living room.
   Find the area of carpet he needs to
   cover the entire living room.

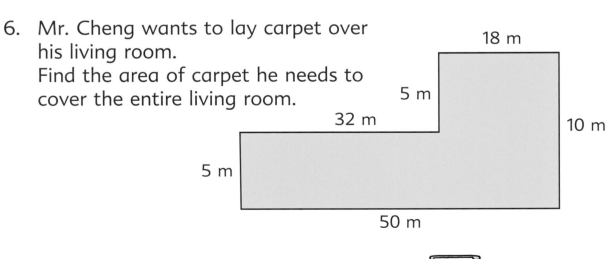

Exercise 7, pages 178—180

1. Find the perimeter of the figure.

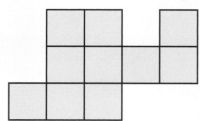

    (A) 10 square units   (B) 17 square units

    (C) 18 square units   (D) 29 square units

2. The area of a square piece of paper is 36 square inches. How long is each side of the square piece of paper?
    (A) 6 in.   (B) 7 in.   (C) 8 in.   (D) 9 in.

3. Adam ran around a rectangular field that was 8 m long and 5 m wide. How far did he run?
    (A) 13 m   (B) 21 m   (C) 26 m   (D) 40 m

4. Select True or False.
   Rectangles with the same perimeter have the same area.   True / False

5. Select True or False.
   Squares with the same perimeter have the same area.   True / False

6.

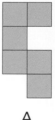   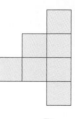   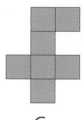

    A   B   C

    (a) Which two figures have the same area?
    (b) Which two figures have the same perimeter?

7.

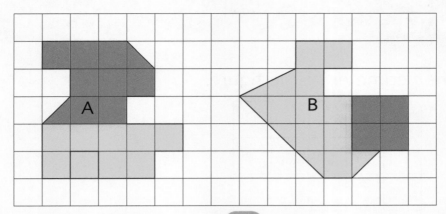

(a) The area of Shape A is [ ] square units.

(b) The area of Shape B is [ ] square units.

(c) Which shape has a greater area, A or B?

(d) What fraction of the units in Shape A are blue?

8.

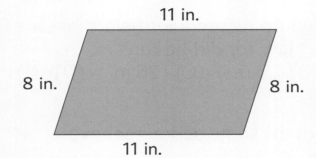

(a) Find the perimeter of this figure.

(b) How many right angles does this figure have?

(c) Is this figure a rhombus?

9. The following figure is made from a square and a rectangle. Find the area and perimeter.

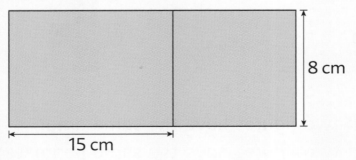

10. The length of a photograph is 15 cm. Its width is 10 cm. Find its area.

11. Evans walked around a rectangular swimming pool.
    The length of the pool is 30 ft.
    Its width is 24 ft.
    How far did he walk?

12. The perimeter of a card is 28 cm.
    Its length is 9 cm.
    Find its width.

13. Fabian cleaned his entire room as shown.
    (a) Find the perimeter of his room.
    (b) Find the area that Fabian cleaned.

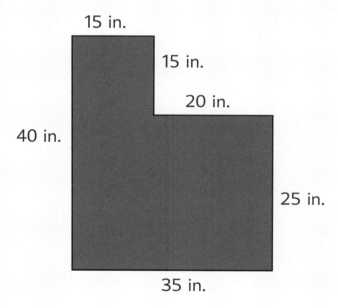

14. Can two rectangles have the same area but different
    perimeters?
    Draw two rectangles to explain your answer.

Review 13, pages 181–183

GLOSSARY

Word	Meaning
A.M.	A.M. is used to tell the time after 12:00 midnight and before 12:00 noon. It is eight o'clock in the morning. The time is 8:00 A.M.
angle	When two straight lines meet, they form an **angle.**
area	The **area** of a figure is the amount of flat space it covers. The area of the above figure is 4 square centimeters.
bar graph	A **bar graph** is a graph that records data using vertical or horizontal rectangular bars.

Word	Meaning
capacity	The **capacity** of a container is the greatest amount it can hold. We measure capacity in liters (L) and milliliters (ml).
cup	The **cup** is a unit of measurement for volume, commonly used in cooking. We write **c** for cup. 1 pint = 2 cups
day	The **day** is a unit of time. 7 days = 1 week
denominator	In the fraction $\frac{1}{2}$, **2** is the **denominator**. $\frac{1}{2}$ ◄—— denominator
equivalent fractions	**Equivalent fractions** are different ways of writing the same fraction. $\frac{1}{3}$ and $\frac{2}{6}$ are equivalent fractions.
gallon	The **gallon** is a unit of measurement for volume. We write **gal** for gallon. 1 gallon = 4 quarts

Word	Meaning
gram	The **gram** is a metric unit of mass. We write **g** for gram. 1,000 grams = 1 kilogram
hexagon	A **hexagon** is a shape with six sides.
hour	The **hour** is a unit of time. We write **h** for hour. From 4:00 to 5:00 is one **hour**. 1 hour = 60 minutes
kilogram	The **kilogram** is a metric unit of mass. We write **kg** for kilogram. 1 kilogram = 1,000 grams
kilometer	The **kilometer** is a metric unit of length used to measure long distances. We write **km** for kilometer. 1 kilometer = 1,000 meters

Word	Meaning
line plot	A **line plot** is a graph that shows how often an event happens.

Word	Meaning
liter	The **liter** is a metric unit of volume. We write **L** for liter. 1 liter = 1,000 milliliters
mass	**Mass** is the amount of matter in an object. Mass can be measured in grams and kilograms.
mile	The **mile** is a unit of length used to measure long distances. We write **mi** for mile. 1 mile = 5,280 feet
milliliter	A **milliliter** is a metric unit of volume. We write **ml** for milliliter. 1,000 milliliters = 1 liter

Word	Meaning
minute	The **minute** is a metric unit of time. We write **min** for minute.

26 minutes later

From 9:30 to 9:56 is 26 minutes later.

60 minutes = 1 hour
1 minute = 60 seconds

Word	Meaning
month	The **month** is a unit of time. 12 months = 1 year
numerator	In the fraction $\frac{1}{2}$, **1** is the **numerator**. $\frac{1}{2}$ ⟵ numerator
octagon	An **octagon** is a shape with eight sides.

Word	Meaning
ounce	The **ounce** is a unit of weight. We write **oz** for ounce. 16 ounces = 1 pound

Word	Meaning
P.M.	**P.M.** is used to tell the time after 12:00 noon and before 12:00 midnight. It is eight o'clock in the evening. The time is 8:00 **P.M.**
pentagon	A **pentagon** is a shape with five sides.
perimeter	The **perimeter** of a figure is the distance around the figure. 4 cm 3 cm 3 cm 2 cm The perimeter of this figure is $4 + 3 + 2 + 3 = 12$ cm.

Word	Meaning
picture graph	A **picture graph** is a graph that records data using pictures or diagrams.
pint	The **pint** is a unit of measurement for volume. We write **pt** for pint. 1 pint = 2 cups 4 pints = 1 quart
pound	A **pound** is a unit of weight. We write **lb** for pound. 1 pound = 16 ounces
quadrilateral	A **quadrilateral** is a shape with four sides. Squares and rectangles are examples of quadrilaterals.

Word	Meaning
quart	The **quart** is a unit of measurement for volume. We write **qt** for quart. 1 quart = 4 cups 4 quarts = 1 gallon
rhombus	A **rhombus** is a quadrilateral that has four equal sides.
right angle	A **right angle** is the angle found in the corners of squares and rectangles.
second	A **second** is a metric unit of time. We write **s** for seconds. 60 seconds = 1 minute
square centimeter	A **square centimeter** is a metric unit of area. It is the same area as a square with 1 cm sides. abbreviation 1 cm / 1 cm

Word	Meaning
square inch	A **square inch** is a unit of area. It is the same area as a square with 1 in. sides. 1 in. 1 in.
unit	A **unit** is an equal part. 1 unit
weight	**Weight** is the pull of gravity on an object. Weight can be measured in pounds and ounces.
week	The **week** is a unit of time. 1 week = 7 days
year	The **year** is a unit of time. 1 year = 12 months or 52 weeks

Grade 3 Curriculum Map

Common Core State Standards		Unit	Student Textbook Pages	Student Workbook Exercises
OPERATIONS AND ALGEBRAIC THINKING				
Represent and solve problems involving multiplication and division.				
3.OA.1	Interpret products of whole numbers, e.g., interpret 5 × 7 as the total number of objects in 5 groups of 7 objects each or 7 groups of 5 objects each. *For example, describe a context in which a total number of objects can be expressed as 5 × 7.*	**Unit 3 Lesson 1 Looking Back** **Unit 4 Lesson 1 Multiplying and Dividing by 6** **Unit 4 Lesson 2 Multiplying and Dividing by 7** **Unit 4 Lesson 3 Multiplying and Dividing by 8** **Unit 4 Lesson 4 Multiplying and Dividing by 9**	**3A:** 79–83, 125–128, 132–135, 138–139, 141–143	**3A:** 75–77, 78–81, 125–126, 127–128, 139–141, 150–151, 152–153, 154–155, 160–161, 162–163, 164–165

Common Core State Standards		Unit	Student Textbook Pages	Student Workbook Exercises
3.OA.2	Interpret whole-number quotients of whole numbers, e.g., interpret 56 ÷ 8 as the number of objects in each share when 56 objects are partitioned equally into 8 shares, or as a number of shares when 56 objects are partitioned into equal shares of 8 objects each. *For example, describe a context in which a number of shares or a number of groups can be expressed as 56 ÷ 8.*	**Unit 3 Lesson 1 Looking Back** **Unit 4 Lesson 1 Multiplying and Dividing by 6** **Unit 4 Lesson 2 Multiplying and Dividing by 7** **Unit 4 Lesson 3 Multiplying and Dividing by 8** **Unit 4 Lesson 4 Multiplying and Dividing by 9**	**3A:** 83–86, 128, 135–136, 139, 143	**3A:** 78–81, 82–85, 125–126, 127–128, 139–141, 142–143, 144–145, 150–151, 152–153, 154–155, 160–161, 162–163, 164–165
3.OA.3	Use multiplication and division within 100 to solve word problems in situations involving equal groups, arrays, and measurement quantities, e.g., by using drawings and equations with a symbol for the unknown number to represent the problem.	**Unit 3 Lesson 1 Looking Back** **Unit 3 Lesson 2 More Word Problems** **Unit 3 Lesson 5 Dividing Hundreds, Tens, and Ones**	**3A:** 88–89, 90–94, 116–117	**3A:** 89–90, 91–93, 114–115

Common Core State Standards		Unit	Student Textbook Pages	Student Workbook Exercises
3.OA.4	Determine the unknown whole number in a multiplication or division equation relating three whole numbers. *For example, determine the unknown number that makes the equation true in each of the equations 8 × ? = 48, 5 = □ ÷ 3, 6 × 6 = ?.*	**Unit 3 Lesson 1 Looking Back** **Unit 3 Lesson 4 Quotient and Remainder** **Unit 3 Lesson 5 Dividing Hundreds, Tens, and Ones**	**3A:** 79–82, 84–86, 105–109, 111, 113–115	**3A:** 75–77, 82–85, 108–109, 112–113
Understand properties of multiplication and the relationship between multiplication and division.				
3.OA.5	Apply properties of operations as strategies to multiply and divide. *Examples: If 6 × 4 = 24 is known, then 4 × 6 = 24 is also known. (Commutative property of multiplication.)* *3 × 5 × 2 can be found by 3 × 5 = 15, then 15 × 2 = 30, or by 5 × 2 = 10, then 3 × 10 = 30. (Associative property of multiplication.)* *Knowing that 8 × 5 = 40 and 8 × 2 = 16, one can find 8 × 7 as 8 × (5 + 2) = (8 × 5) + (8 × 2) = 40 + 16 = 56. (Distributive property.)*	**Unit 3 Lesson 1 Looking Back** **Unit 4 Lesson 1 Multiplying and Dividing by 6** **Unit 4 Lesson 2 Multiplying and Dividing by 7** **Unit 4 Lesson 3 Multiplying and Dividing by 8** **Unit 4 Lesson 4 Multiplying and Dividing by 9**	**3A:** 80, 82–83, 85, 126–127, 133–134, 138, 141, 143	**3A:** 75–77, 78–81, 160–161, 162–163, 164–165

Common Core State Standards		Unit	Student Textbook Pages	Student Workbook Exercises
3.OA.6	Understand division as an unknown-factor problem. *For example, find 32 ÷ 8 by finding the number that makes 32 when multiplied by 8.*	**Unit 3** **Lesson 1** **Looking Back** **Unit 4** **Lesson 1** **Multiplying and Dividing by 6** **Unit 4** **Lesson 2** **Multiplying and Dividing by 7**	**3A:** 85, 128, 135	**3A:** 125–126, 127–128, 139–141
Multiply and divide within 100.				
3.OA.7	Fluently multiply and divide within 100, using strategies such as the relationship between multiplication and division (e.g., knowing that 8 × 5 = 40, one knows 40 ÷ 5 = 8) or properties of operations. By the end of Grade 3, know from memory all products of two one-digit numbers.	**Unit 3** **Lesson 1** **Looking Back** **Unit 3** **Lesson 3** **Multiplying Ones, Tens, and Hundreds** **Unit 3 Lesson 4** **Quotient and Remainder** **Unit 3 Lesson 5** **Dividing Hundreds, Tens, and Ones** **Unit 4** **Lesson 1** **Multiplying and Dividing by 6** **Unit 4** **Lesson 2** **Multiplying and Dividing by 7** **Unit 4** **Lesson 3** **Multiplying and Dividing by 8** **Unit 4 Lesson 4** **Multiplying and Dividing by 9**	**3A:** 86–87, 89, 97, 100, 110, 114, 115, 117, 128, 130, 135–136, 139, 143	**3A:** 82–85, 86–88, 89–90, 97–98, 101–103, 110–111, 112–113, 114–115, 125–126, 127–128, 132–134, 139–141, 142–143, 144–145, 150–151, 152–153, 154–155, 160–161, 162–163, 164–165

Common Core State Standards		Unit	Student Textbook Pages	Student Workbook Exercises
Solve problems involving the four operations, and identify and explain patterns in arithmetic.				
3.OA.8	Solve two-step word problems using the four operations. Represent these problems using equations with a letter standing for the unknown quantity. Assess the reasonableness of answers using mental computation and estimation strategies including rounding.	**Unit 2 Lesson 7 Two-Step Word Problems** **Unit 3 Lesson 2 More Word Problems** **Unit 3 Lesson 5 Dividing Hundreds, Tens, and Ones** **Unit 4 Lesson 2 Multiplying and Dividing by 7** **Unit 4 Lesson 4 Multiplying and Dividing by 9** **Unit 6 Lesson 5 Word Problems**	**3A:** 66–69, 92–94, 117, 137, 144 **3B:** 26–28	**3A:** 65–67, 91–93, 114–115, 146–149, 166–169 **3B:** 24–26

Common Core State Standards		Unit	Student Textbook Pages	Student Workbook Exercises
3.OA.9	Identify arithmetic patterns (including patterns in the addition table or multiplication table), and explain them using properties of operations. *For example, observe that 4 times a number is always even, and explain why 4 times a number can be decomposed into two equal addends.*	**Unit 1 Lesson 1 Thousands, Hundreds, Tens, and Ones** **Unit 1 Lesson 2 Number Patterns** **Unit 2 Lesson 1 Mental Calculation** **Unit 3 Lesson 1 Looking Back** **Unit 4 Lesson 1 Multiplying and Dividing by 6** **Unit 4 Lesson 2 Multiplying and Dividing by 7** **Unit 4 Lesson 3 Multiplying and Dividing by 8** **Unit 4 Lesson 4 Multiplying and Dividing by 9**	**3A:** 8–11, 15–17, 29–33, 78–84, 122–123, 126–128, 133–135, 138, 139, 141–143	**3A:** 6–8, 13–15, 28-29, 30, 31–32, 75–77, 78–81, 125–126, 127–128, 139–141, 150–151, 152–153, 154–155, 160–161, 162–163, 164–165

Common Core State Standards		Unit	Student Textbook Pages	Student Workbook Exercises
NUMBER AND OPERATIONS IN BASE TEN				
Use place value understanding and properties of operations to perform multi-digit arithmetic.				
3.NBT.1	Use place value understanding to round whole numbers to the nearest 10 or 100.	**Unit 1 Lesson 3 Rounding Numbers** **Unit 2 Lesson 5 Adding Ones, Tens, Hundreds, and Thousands** **Unit 3 Lesson 3 Multiplying Ones, Tens, and Hundreds** **Unit 4 Lesson 1 Multiplying and Dividing by 6**	**3A:** 18–23, 53, 102–103, 129	**3A:** 16–17, 18–19, 53–54, 104–105, 129–131

Common Core State Standards		Unit	Student Textbook Pages	Student Workbook Exercises
3.NBT.2	Fluently add and subtract within 1,000 using strategies and algorithms based on place value, properties of operations, and/or the relationship between addition and subtraction.	**Unit 1 Lesson 1 Thousands, Hundreds, Tens, and Ones** **Unit 1 Lesson 2 Number Patterns** **Unit 2 Lesson 1 Mental Calculation** **Unit 2 Lesson 2 Looking Back: Addition and Subtraction** **Unit 2 Lesson 3 Sum and Difference** **Unit 2 Lesson 4 Word Problems** **Unit 2 Lesson 5 Adding Ones, Tens, Hundreds, and Thousands** **Unit 2 Lesson 6 Subtracting Ones, Tens, Hundreds, and Thousands** **Unit 5 Lesson 1 Meters and Centimeters** **Unit 5 Lesson 2 Kilometers** **Unit 5 Lesson 3 Other Units of Length**	**3A:** 8–12, 15–17, 29–35, 36–38, 39–44, 45–49, 50–56, 57–65, 151–152, 157–162, 164–167	**3A:** 6–8, 9–10, 13–15, 28–29, 30, 31–32, 33, 34–35, 36–37, 38–39, 40–41, 42–43, 44, 45–47, 48–50, 51–52, 53–54, 55–56, 57–58, 59–60, 61–62, 63–64, 176–177, 181–184, 185–186, 187–189, 190, 191–192

Common Core State Standards		Unit	Student Textbook Pages	Student Workbook Exercises
3.NBT.3	Multiply one-digit whole numbers by multiples of 10 in the range 10–90 (e.g., 9 × 80, 5 × 60) using strategies based on place value and properties of operations.	**Unit 3 Lesson 3 Multiplying Ones, Tens, and Hundreds**	**3A:** 96–99, 101	**3A:** 97–98, 99–100
NUMBER AND OPERATIONS—FRACTIONS				
Develop understanding of fractions as numbers.				
3.NF.1	Understand a fraction $1/b$ as the quantity formed by 1 part when a whole is partitioned into b equal parts; understand a fraction a/b as the quantity formed by a parts of size $1/b$.	**Unit 9 Lesson 1 Fraction of a Whole** **Unit 9 Lesson 4 Fraction of a Set**	**3B:** 85–86, 103–106	**3B:** 83–86, 107–108, 109–110
3.NF.2a	Understand a fraction as a number on the number line; represent fractions on a number line diagram. Represent a fraction $1/b$ on a number line diagram by defining the interval from 0 to 1 as the whole and partitioning it into b equal parts. Recognize that each part has size $1/b$ and that the endpoint of the part based at 0 locates the number $1/b$ on the number line.	**Unit 9 Lesson 1 Fraction of a Whole**	**3B:** 90	**3B:** 89–93
3.NF.2b	Understand a fraction as a number on the number line; represent fractions on a number line diagram. Represent a fraction a/b on a number line diagram by marking off a lengths $1/b$ from 0. Recognize that the resulting interval has size a/b and that its endpoint locates the number a/b on the number line.	**Unit 9 Lesson 1 Fraction of a Whole**	**3B:** 90	**3B:** 89–93
3.NF.3a	Explain equivalence of fractions in special cases, and compare fractions by reasoning about their size. Understand two fractions as equivalent (equal) if they are the same size, or the same point on a number line.	**Unit 9 Lesson 2 Equivalent Fractions**	**3B:** 92–94	**3B:** 94–96

Common Core State Standards		Unit	Student Textbook Pages	Student Workbook Exercises
3.NF.3b	Explain equivalence of fractions in special cases, and compare fractions by reasoning about their size. Recognize and generate simple equivalent fractions, e.g., 1/2 = 2/4, 4/6 = 2/3. Explain why the fractions are equivalent, e.g., by using a visual fraction model.	**Unit 9 Lesson 2 Equivalent Fractions**	**3B:** 95–97	**3B:** 97–98, 99–100, 101–102
3.NF.3c	Explain equivalence of fractions in special cases, and compare fractions by reasoning about their size. Express whole numbers as fractions, and recognize fractions that are equivalent to whole numbers. *Examples: Express 3 in the form 3 = 3/1; recognize that 6/1 = 6; locate 4/4 and 1 at the same point of a number line diagram.*	**Unit 9 Lesson 2 Equivalent Fractions**	**3B:** 94, 95	**3B:** 97–98
3.NF.3d	Explain equivalence of fractions in special cases, and compare fractions by reasoning about their size. Compare two fractions with the same numerator or the same denominator by reasoning about their size. Recognize that comparisons are valid only when the two fractions refer to the same whole. Record the results of comparisons with the symbols >, =, or <, and justify the conclusions, e.g., by using a visual fraction model.	**Unit 9 Lesson 2 Equivalent Fractions**	**3B:** 97–98	**3B:** 103
MEASUREMENT AND DATA				
Solve problems involving measurement and estimation of intervals of time, liquid volumes, and masses of objects.				
3.MD.1	Tell and write time to the nearest minute and measure time intervals in minutes. Solve word problems involving addition and subtraction of time intervals in minutes, e.g., by representing the problem on a number line diagram.	**Unit 10 Lesson 1 Hours and Minutes**	**3B:** 113–121	**3B:** 115–116, 117–118, 119–120, 121–122, 123–124, 125–126

Common Core State Standards		Unit	Student Textbook Pages	Student Workbook Exercises
3.MD.2	Measure and estimate liquid volumes and masses of objects using standard units of grams (g), kilograms (kg), and liters (l). Add, subtract, multiply, or divide to solve one-step word problems involving masses or volumes that are given in the same units, e.g., by using drawings (such as a beaker with a measurement scale) to represent the problem.	**Unit 6 Lesson 2 Measuring Mass in Kilograms** **Unit 6 Lesson 3 Measuring Mass in Grams** **Unit 6 Lesson 4 Kilograms and Grams** **Unit 6 Lesson 5 Word Problems** **Unit 7 Lesson 1 Comparing Capacity** **Unit 7 Lesson 2 Liters** **Unit 7 Lesson 3 Liters and Milliliters** **Unit 7 Lesson 4 Gallons, Quarts, Pints, and Cups**	**3B:** 10–14, 15–19, 20–24, 25–28, 41–62	**3B:** 9–12, 17, 18–20, 21–23, 24–26, 37–39, 40, 41–44, 45–46, 47–48, 49–53, 54–55, 56–57, 58

Common Core State Standards		Unit	Student Textbook Pages	Student Workbook Exercises
Represent and interpret data.				
3.MD.3	Draw a scaled picture graph and a scaled bar graph to represent a data set with several categories. Solve one- and two-step "how many more" and "how many less" problems using information presented in scaled bar graphs. *For example, draw a bar graph in which each square in the bar graph might represent 5 pets.*	**Unit 11 Lesson 1 Presenting Data**	**3B:** 129–132	**3B:** 138–144
3.MD.4	Generate measurement data by measuring lengths using rulers marked with halves and fourths of an inch. Show the data by making a line plot, where the horizontal scale is marked off in appropriate units—whole numbers, halves, or quarters.	**Unit 11 Lesson 1 Presenting Data**	**3B:** 133	**3B:** 145–146
Geometric measurement: understand concepts of area and relate area to multiplication and to addition.				
3.MD.5a	Recognize area as an attribute of plane figures and understand concepts of area measurement. A square with side length 1 unit, called "a unit square," is said to have "one square unit" of area, and can be used to measure area.	**Unit 13 Lesson 1 Area**	**3B:** 144–147	**3B:** 158–161, 162–166
3.MD.5b	Recognize area as an attribute of plane figures and understand concepts of area measurement. A plane figure which can be covered without gaps or overlaps by *n* unit squares is said to have an area of *n* square units.	**Unit 13 Lesson 1 Area** **Unit 13 Lesson 3 Area of a Rectangle** **Unit 13 Lesson 4 Composite Figures**	**3B:** 144–151, 157–160, 161–164	**3B:** 158–161, 162–166, 167–170, 175–177, 178–180

Common Core State Standards		Unit	Student Textbook Pages	Student Workbook Exercises
3.MD.6	Measure areas by counting unit squares (square cm, square m, square in., square ft, and improvised units).	**Unit 13 Lesson 1 Area**	**3B:** 144 –150	**3B:** 158–161, 162–166, 167–170
3.MD.7a	Relate area to the operations of multiplication and addition. Find the area of a rectangle with whole-number side lengths by tiling it, and show that the area is the same as would be found by multiplying the side lengths.	**Unit 13 Lesson 3 Area of a Rectangle**	**3B:** 157–158	
3.MD.7b	Relate area to the operations of multiplication and addition. Multiply side lengths to find areas of rectangles with whole-number side lengths in the context of solving real world and mathematical problems, and represent whole-number products as rectangular areas in mathematical reasoning.	**Unit 13 Lesson 3 Area of a Rectangle**	**3B:** 159–160	**3B:** 175–177
3.MD.7c	Relate area to the operations of multiplication and addition. Use tiling to show in a concrete case that the area of a rectangle with whole-number side lengths a and $b + c$ is the sum of $a \times b$ and $a \times c$. Use area models to represent the distributive property in mathematical reasoning.	**Unit 13 Lesson 4 Composite Figures**	**3B:** 163	
3.MD.7d	Relate area to the operations of multiplication and addition. Recognize area as additive. Find areas of rectilinear figures by decomposing them into non-overlapping rectangles and adding the areas of the non-overlapping parts, applying this technique to solve real world problems.	**Unit 13 Lesson 4 Composite Figures**	**3B:** 164	**3B:** 178–180

Common Core State Standards		Unit	Student Textbook Pages	Student Workbook Exercises
Geometric measurement: recognize perimeter as an attribute of plane figures and distinguish between linear and area measures.				
3.MD.8	Solve real world and mathematical problems involving perimeters of polygons, including finding the perimeter given the side lengths, finding an unknown side length, and exhibiting rectangles with the same perimeter and different areas or with the same area and different perimeters.	**Unit 13 Lesson 2 Perimeter** **Unit 13 Lesson 4 Composite Figures**	**3B:** 153–156, 161	**3B:** 171–172, 173–174
GEOMETRY				
Reason with shapes and their attributes.				
3.G.1	Understand that shapes in different categories (e.g., rhombuses, rectangles, and others) may share attributes (e.g., having four sides), and that the shared attributes can define a larger category (e.g., quadrilaterals). Recognize rhombuses, rectangles, and squares as examples of quadrilaterals, and draw examples of quadrilaterals that do not belong to any of these subcategories.	**Unit 12 Lesson 1 Right Angles and Shapes**	**3B:** 140	**3B:** 153–155
3.G.2	Partition shapes into parts with equal areas. Express the area of each part as a unit fraction of the whole. *For example, partition a shape into 4 parts with equal area, and describe the area of each part as 1/4 of the area of the shape.*	**Unit 9 Lesson 1 Fraction of a Whole**	**3B:** 86–89	**3B:** 83–88

Index

BLANK